PURPLE GOLDFISH

FRANCHISE EDITION

THE ULTIMATE S.Y.S.T.E.M.
FOR FRANCHISORS AND FRANCHISEES

STAN PHELPS
&
TIFFANY W. DODSON

Published by 9 INCH MARKETING, LLC, Cary, NC

Copyeditor: Lee Heinrich
Cover and Layout: Evan Carroll

Ordering Information:

Special discounts are available on quantity purchases by corporations, associations, and others. For details, please contact stan@purplegoldfish.com

First Edition

ISBN: 978-1-7326652-1-7

1. Business. 2. Marketing 3. Customer Experience 4. Franchising

First Printing: 2018

Printed and bound in the United States of America

This book is dedicated to my beautiful wife, Jenn,
and our two boys, Thomas and James.
Their support and love made the original
Purple Goldfish Project possible.

—Stan Phelps

This book is dedicated to my husband Ryan Dodson,
our two daughters Willard and Ritter
as well as my mother, Jeanne Willard.

For some reason, you all think that I am Wonder Woman
and your belief in my ability carries me a long way.

A thank you as well to my co-author, Stan Phelps,
for being my book-writing Sherpa.

And acknowledgement to three of my early business mentors:
Willie Baker, Mark Suter, and John Hewitt.
Thank you for your generous mentorship.
Your lessons have helped me for many years.

—Tiffany W. Dodson

ACKNOWLEDGEMENTS

We'd like to thank everyone who inspired us, supported us, or provided feedback and examples for the book:

Susan Adams, James Allen, Aaron Bakke, Liz Barrett, Julie Bennett, Pete Blackshaw, Brad Bossow, Rhonda Byrne, Jim Collins, Evan Carroll, Bill Chemero, Dean Clarino, Brandon Cook, Jarvis Cromwell, Dean Crutchfield, Jason Daly, Faye Davis, Hank Davis, Michael Debenham, Ryan Dodson, John Eucalitto, Debbie Fiorina, Hershey H. Friedman, Milton Friedman, Bob Gappa, Pam Gappa, Keith Gerson, Phil Gerbyshak, Malcolm Gladwell, Seth Godin, Sam Gordon, Brad Griswold, Barney Hamilton, Lee Heinrich, David Hines, Lewis Hyde, Erich Joachimsthaler, Mark Johnson, Tim Johnson, Daniel Kahneman, Steve Knox, Bill Kraus, Debi Lane, Ted Levitt, Rod Lowe, Glenn Mathijssen, Jerry Murrell, Martha O'Gorman, Mark O'Neill, Greg Nathan, Steve Newton, Les Perkins, Jennifer Phelps, Steve Pinetti, Whitney Preslar, Ahmed Rahman, Frederick Reichheld, Alexei Romanov, John Romero, Mark Siebert, Doug Smith, Susan Smith, Susan Sontag, Joe Sorge, Roger Staubach, W. Clement Stone, Steve Strauss, Jeff Summers, Mary Thompson, Michael Thrasher, Pete Tucker, Mark Twain, Karlton Utter, Kevin von Duuglas-ittu , Kristen Von Tersch, Mike Weinberger, Pat Williams, Kevin Wilson, and Chris Zane

CONTENTS

FOREWORD

BY BOB GAPPA

"Knowledge has to be improved, challenged, and increased constantly, or it vanishes."

- Peter Drucker

When I started Management 2000 in 1981 I established our Mission as: "To give people what they expect and more." This conveys what we are committed to doing with: our internal team members, strangers, clients, family, neighbors, everyone. To do this you must first listen so you know what they expect (i.e. some help getting their luggage in the overhead bin on the airplane) or (getting a franchisee to comply for the right motivations), and then achieve their result and more. I was developed, as a consultant, to "always leave a client with unexpected value."

Over the last 30 years, I have witnessed changes in the ways franchising is used as a business strategy. In the 20th century, franchisees believed they owned their franchise and franchisors often considered franchisees as the customer. Now in the 21st century, franchisors see franchisees as their Strategic-Partners working collaboratively to create and retain very satisfied, loyal, frequent user customers who recommend them to their friends and family. They achieve this by creating experiences for team members and customers making both want to come back. This is accomplished by bringing personal passion for creating great experiences by following the operating SYSTEM that makes the franchised Brand recognized and loved.

Because of Brand recognition, customers develop certain expectations, about the quality of the product, the caliber of service, the professionalism of the staff, and so on. The objective for a franchise company is to meet these expectations by managing them. Every time. The way they do this is through consistent application of the same operating SYSTEM, wherever a unit is located. An operating SYSTEM is a way of doing business that, over time, proves (or disproves) it can work. When everyone in the system, everywhere in the country, is following the operating SYSTEM, the public's experience is reinforced. They come to understand there will be no surprises when they buy. They know they'll receive the same quality and service, no matter which office they call, or store they shop, or service they buy. It is in every franchise's best interest to observe the operating system, every time. Not just the first time, or not just until they "have it down," but every time, not for their sake, but for the customer's sake, because it fulfills the buyer's expectation. Following the operating SYSTEM increases the value of the Brand because every time a customer has an experience with it, it's positive. It is also important that within the franchise system, every franchise has confidence that everyone else in the system is conducting business in exactly the same way, so anyone who uses your services, no matter where they are located, has the same experience with every Unit they frequent.

To improve and continue to grow, there must be a way to measure the standards that contribute success at the unit level and at the franchisor level so that knowledge is harvested and shared across the system. Growth comes from identifying opportunities to serve the customer not only better than the competition, but also with a point of difference that creates an emotional bond. This requires discovering where opportunities lie, designing a plan to improve and then deploying it to your Strategic-Partners.

Purple Goldfish, Franchise Edition, leaves the reader with unexpected value. The authors, Stan and Tiffany, researched numerous examples to construct a way of looking at franchises, a SYSTEM, that focuses on the end customer and how franchises create an emotional connection with the customer, so that the customer chooses the same business again and again. Using this lens, the authors offer several examples for each concept that illustrates ways that franchisors and franchisees excel in their industry by delighting more customers every day with unexpected value. To identify areas to improve, the authors include a section to discover opportunities to improve, design an improvement plan and suggestions on deploying so that the book examples provide actionable learning that will grow your franchise.

INTRODUCTION

BY STAN PHELPS

"The difference between ordinary and extraordinary ...is just a little extra."

- W. Clement Stone

CAN LITTLE THINGS MAKE A BIG DIFFERENCE?

A number of years ago an experiment was conducted in a quick serve restaurant. The objective of the study by Hershey H. Friedman and Ahmed Rahman was to determine the effects of reciprocity in business. Specifically, how giving a small gift upon entry and greeting customers with a thank you for their patronage will impact performance. Two types of gifts were used in the experiment. Some customers received a cup of yogurt and some were given an inexpensive keychain. To study the impact on sales, satisfaction, and recommendations, the experiment created four groups of customers:

1. Group #1 (the control group) did not receive a greeting upon entry nor a gift.

2. Group #2 received a greeting upon entry but were not given a gift.

3. Group #3 received both a greeting upon entry and a gift of a key chain.

4. Group #4 received both a greeting upon entry and a gift of a yogurt sample.

HOW BIG WAS THE IMPACT?

In Group #1, customers who were not greeted nor given a gift spent $7.11 on average. Group #2 customers with only the greeting upon entry spent $8.39 on average. Group #3, those with the greeting and the key chain, spent $9.39 on average. Group #4 that received both an appreciatory greeting and a cup of yogurt upon entry spent on average $10.41. That was 46.4% higher than the control group, a considerable increase in sales.

The article was published in International *Journal of Marketing Studies*[1]. The study demonstrates that there is value in greeting customers who enter a store. Customers who are not greeted will spend considerably less, will rate the store lower on performance, and will also be less likely to recommend the establishment. Providing a small gift upon entry into a store will have an impact on how much is spent, on the performance rating, and on how strongly the establishment will be recommended. Little things systematically done can truly make a big difference.

THE ORIGIN OF THE PURPLE GOLDFISH

In 2012, the original book, *Purple Goldfish - How to Win Customers and Influence Word of Mouth,* was released. It was the culmination of a 27-month crowdsourcing effort called the Purple Goldfish Project. The Project looked at over 1,000 examples of how companies could do the little extras to stand out in a crowded marketplace.

---

1. http://www.onefiftynine.com/assets/File/Blog%20Downloads/Customer%20Loyalty%20Research.pdf.

In 2013, I made the leap to be a full-time author and speaker. My first two clients were two franchise organizations: Better Homes & Garden Real Estate and Liberty Tax Service. Over the last five years, I've had the opportunity to share the Goldfish message with thousands of companies at over 300 events on every inhabited continent. Many of those organizations leverage a franchise business model.

Purple Goldfish was followed by six additional colors in the Series: *Green Goldfish* (Employee Engagement), *Golden Goldfish* (Top Customers/Employees), *Blue Goldfish* (Technology), *Red Goldfish* (Purpose), *Pink Goldfish* (Differentiation), and *Yellow Goldfish* (Happiness). They all explore little ways to drive differentiation, increase loyalty, and promote word of mouth in business. It is a strong fit for franchise businesses. Franchisors and franchisees have a similar goal. In the words of franchise expert Bob Gappa, "[It] is a strategic alliance between groups of people who have specific relationships and responsibilities with a common goal to dominate markets, i.e., to get and keep more customers than their competitors."

In 2015, I had the opportunity to meet Tiffany W. Dodson at the Liberty Tax International Conference. Tiffany entered franchising after a successful career in brand marketing with Phillip Morris, Miller Coors, and Krispy Kreme. As both a franchisee and an area developer and trainer, she has created a track record of distinction. She was voted by her peers to be the Master Developer, not once but twice with Liberty Tax Service. In the span of eight years, Tiffany grew her master franchise areas from four to 90 locations.

Although the original *Purple Goldfish* was written about customer experience, the same principles apply to franchisees as well as customers. This book will look at both in five parts:

Part One of this book will provide background on the concept of a Purple Goldfish. Tiffany and I were interested in examining how successful franchisors were able to create scalable systems.

In 2017, we launched the Purple Goldfish Franchise Project on Listly[2]. The result is the S.Y.S.T.E.M. framework we will share in **Part Two** of this book. **Part Three** will focus on the how of creating your own Purple Goldfish. **Part Four** will distill the top five takeaways. The final section, **Part Five**, will share some bonus content about the Purple Goldfish and provide some recommendations for additional reading and inspiration.

In *Purple Goldfish Franchise Edition,* Tiffany W. Dodson and I are asking you to consider the long term—to intentionally touch the hearts and minds of the franchisees and customers that you serve on a daily basis. This book will show you proven strategies, ideas, and anecdotes that you can leverage and apply in your own franchise. At the end of the day, it's difficult to quantify the impact of genuinely serving others and creating a remarkable experience. However, what we're advocating is the willingness to try and adapt to today's business landscape and allocate the resources necessary. Be willing and able to test, fail, and continually improve. Your franchisees and customers are counting on you.

2. https://list.ly/list/1boV-purple-goldfish-franchise-edition

PREFACE

"In marketing, I've seen only one strategy that can't miss - and that is to market to your best customers first, your best prospects second, and the rest of the world last."

—John Romero

Here are the top 10 ways that marketing is changing and impacting franchising:

10. Retention is becoming the new acquisition. It now costs up to 10 times the amount of money to acquire a new customer than it does to keep a current one[1].

9. Word of mouth is golden. 90% of customers identify word of mouth as the best, most reliable, trustworthy source about ideas and information on products or services[2].

8. Consumers are tuned out to traditional media. Nearly 84% of consumers say that they fast forward through TV commercials or leave the room when commercials are on[3].

7. Competition is steadily increasing, and there is always an alternative. Over 78% of consumers will abandon a brand because of a bad customer experience[4].

---

1. http://bit.ly/ForbesRetention
2. http://www.businessweek.com/debateroom/archives/2011/12/word_of_mouth_is_the_best_ad.html
3. http://blogs.wsj.com/cmo/2014/05/28/whythec3vc7debateintvadvertisingmaybeirrelevant
4. https://www.helpscout.net/75customerservicefactsquotesstatistics

6. Consumers may not know what they like... but they like what they know or what their network knows. According to McKinsey, 67% of all consumer decisions are primarily influenced by word of mouth[5].

5. Interruption marketing has run amuck. In the 1970s, the average consumer was exposed to 500 to 2,000 messages per day. Today, consumers are approached with 3,000 to 5,000 messages per day[6]. How do you expect to break through all of that noise?

4. Love is a battlefield for customers and marketing. Survey says: 94% of business leaders say customer experience is the new battlefield[7].

3. Forget the water cooler. The online social landscape has become a game changer. According to author Pete Blackshaw, "Today's satisfied customer tells three friends, an upset customer tells 3,000[8]."

2. Double the pleasure in marketing. Customers gained through word of mouth have up to 2 times the lifetime value of regular customers[9]. They also bring in up to twice the number of referrals.

1. Customer experience reigns supreme. According to Gartner, "89 percent of companies expect to compete mostly on the basis of customer service. Six years ago, this number was 36 percent[10]."

---

5. http://bit.ly/McKinseyExperience
6. http://sjinsights.net/2014/09/29/newresearchshedslightondailyadexposures
7. http://www.infor.com/content/pitfalls/thinkyourcustomersarehavinggreatexperiences.pdf
8. http://bit.ly/AngryCustomersBlackshaw
9. http://www.bain.com/publications/articles/theeconomicsofloyalty.aspx
10. http://blogs.gartner.com/jakesorofman/gartnersurveysconfirmcustomerexperiencenewbattlefield

PART I

THE CASE FOR DIFFERENTIATION

CHAPTER 1

THE BIGGEST MYTH IN MARKETING

"The search for meaningful distinction is central to the marketing effort. If marketing is about anything, it is about achieving customer-getting distinction by differentiating what you do and how you operate. All else is derivative of that and only that."

—Theodore Levitt

TALL TALES FROM NYC

In the summer of 2009, Stan was in New York City with a work colleague at a trendy rooftop bar. One of those places where a bottle of beer costs $15. They were waiting to meet a few people before heading over to a networking event, and Stan noticed an older gentleman sitting on his own for over 30 minutes. Every so often he would look around the bar. It was obvious he was waiting for someone. Stan decided to strike up a conversation about waiting by offering his standard line, "Did you know that we spend 10% of our life waiting?"

The new acquaintance and Stan started talking about waiting. Stan stressed the importance of being on time. As soon as Stan said this, the "waiting man" (as he is now known) shook his head in disagreement and said something that Stan will never forget. The man said, "There is no such thing as being on time. Being on time is a fallacy. You either are early...or you are late. No one is ever on time. Being 'on time' is a myth."

This was a complete paradigm shift for Stan. He immediately started thinking about how this principle applies to marketing and meeting customer expectations. Stan has always thought that the idea of meeting expectations was a surefire recipe for losing business. Merely meeting expectations almost always guarantees that you will fall short. It's similar to playing "prevent" defense in football. Prevent defense only prevents you from doing one thing...winning.

This new paradigm has only made it clearer for us. Meeting expectations is the biggest myth in business. Santa Claus, the Tooth Fairy, and "meeting expectations" all have something in common. Kids, cover your eyes and ears...they are all myths.

In business, you either fall below expectations or you exceed them. There is no middle ground. It bears repeating, "There is no such thing as meeting expectations." In a world where 60 to 80 percent of customers describe their customer satisfaction as satisfied or very satisfied before going on to defect to other brands, "meeting expectations" is no longer an option. As a franchisor, you deal with expectations from both customers *and* franchisees.

CHOOSE YOUR PATH WISELY

There are two paths that diverge in the corporate woods. Many companies take the wide first path and are happy with just meeting expectations. Others consciously take the narrower and tougher road deciding to go above and beyond to do more than reasonably expected.

Author Seth Godin wrote about under promising and over delivering in a post entitled, "Once in a Lifetime."[1] Seth touches on these two paths:

> This is perhaps the greatest marketing strategy struggle of our time: Should your product or service be very good, meet spec and be beyond reproach or...should it be a remarkable, memorable, over the top, a tell-your-friends event?
>
> The answer isn't obvious, and many organizations are really conflicted about this. Delta Airlines isn't trying to make your day. They're trying to get you from Atlanta to Salt Lake City, close to on time, less expensive than the other guy and hopefully without hassle. That's a win for them.
>
> Most of the consumer businesses (restaurants, services, etc.) and virtually all of the business to busi-

1. http://sethgodin.typepad.com/seths_blog/2010/02/once-in-a-lifetime.html

> ness ventures I encounter, shoot for the first (meeting spec). They define spec and they work to achieve it. A few, from event organizers to investment advisors, work every single day to create over-the-top remarkable experiences. It's a lot of work, and it requires passion.

You can't be all things to all people. Your strategy defines which path you will take, but it's important that you don't get caught in the mushy middle. It boils down to the simple issue of meeting expectations. If all you want to do is meet expectations, then you are setting yourself up to become a commodity. If you are not willing to differentiate yourself by creating valuable experiences or little touches that go "above and beyond" for your franchisees and customers, then you will languish in the sea of sameness. Choose your path wisely.

TO UNDER-DELIVER OR OVER-DELIVER?

In today's climate, you need to stand out by answering two important questions:

1. What makes you different?

2. *Are those differentiators signature elements to your franchise?*

Creating small unexpected extras can go a long way toward increasing retention, promoting loyalty, and generating positive word of mouth. Investing your marketing budget in current franchisees and customers is the lowest hanging fruit in marketing. Focusing solely on prospective franchisees and neglecting actual customer experience is a recipe for disaster.

SHAREHOLDERS VS. CUSTOMERS

Stan's friend, Jarvis Cromwell, of *Reputation Garage,* asked an interesting question, "Why are corporations in business?" He proposed that there are two sides of the argument:

1. Milton Friedman's theory that the sole purpose of a corporation is to drive shareholder value. Friedman said, "There is one and only one social responsibility of business, and that is to engage in activities designed to increase profits."[2]

2. The late American economist and professor at Harvard Business School, Theodore "Ted" Levitt, offered a different theory that states that companies are solely in the business of getting and keeping customers. Levitt said, "Not so long ago companies assumed the purpose of a business is to make money. But that has proved as vacuous as saying the purpose of life is to eat...The purpose of a business is to create and keep a customer."[3]

What comes first then: the customer or the bottom line? The last 100 years have seen corporations solely focused on the bottom line. The approach has been to win at all costs with little or no regard to external effects, collateral damage or customer experience. The problem is that only pursuing the bottom line often neglects the customer. This was outlined in an article from Harvard Business School by James Allen, Frederick Reichheld, and Barney Hamilton:[4]

> Call it the dominance trap: The larger a company's market share, the greater the risk it will take its customers for granted. As the money flows in, manage-

---

2. http://www.colorado.edu/studentgroups/libertarians/issues/friedman-soc-resp-business.html
3. http://dwgreen.com/2015/06/the-purpose-of-a-business-is-to-get-and-keep-a-customer
4. http://hbswk.hbs.edu/archive/5075.html

> ment begins confusing customer profitability with customer loyalty, never realizing that the most lucrative buyers may also be the angriest and most alienated. Worse, traditional market research may lead the firm to view customers as statistics. Managers can become so focused on the data that they stop hearing the real voices of their customers.

The entire premise of *Purple Goldfish Franchise Edition* is that franchisees and customers must come first. Their experience should be priority number one. It's essential that you stop focusing all of your energy on "the two in the bush" (your prospects) and start taking better care of "the one in your hand" (your current franchisees and customers).

VALUE IS THE NEW BLACK

In challenging economic times, the business climate often forces both brands and consumers toward a "value" model. Plain and simple, consumers are expecting more value from you. According to the Brand Keys Customer Loyalty Index,[5] successful brands are those that stand out because consumers think of them as valuable. Please be aware that we are not advocating consumers as using the term "value" synonymously for "cheap." Brand Keys analyzed consumer values, needs, and expectations and offered the following trends:

1. Value is the new black: Consumer spending, even on sale items, will continue to be replaced by a "reason to buy" at all. This may spell trouble for brands with no authentic meaning, whether high or low-end products or services.

---

5. http://brandkeys.com/portfolio/customerloyaltyengagementindex

2. Brand differentiation is brand value: The unique meaning of a brand will increase in importance as generic features continue to propagate in the brand landscape. Awareness as a meaningful market force has long been obsolete, and differentiation will be critical for sales and profitability.

3. Consumer expectations are growing: Brands are barely keeping up with consumer expectations now. Every day consumers adopt and devour the latest technologies and innovations, and they hunger for still more. Smarter marketers will identify and capitalize on unmet expectations. Those brands that understand where the strongest expectations exist will be the brands that not only survive but prosper.

4. It's not just buzz: Conversation and community are increasingly important. If consumers trust the community, they will extend trust to the brand. This means not just word of mouth, but the right word of mouth within the community. This has significant implications for the future of customer service.

5. Consumers talk with each other before talking with brands: Social networking and exchange of information outside of the brand space will increase. This—at least in theory—will mean more opportunities for brands to get involved in these spaces and meet customers where they are.

THE SEA OF SAMENESS

This all begs the question, "How do you stand out in a sea of sameness?" What are your signature differentiators in customer and franchisee experience? Instead of being a "me too," what are the special things your company does that are superior and distinctive in the eyes of franchisees and customers?

What is that little something extra that is tangible, valuable, and talkable? How do you stand out from your competition? In other words, "What's your Purple Goldfish?"

CHAPTER 2

WHY A GOLDFISH?

"The thing that makes something remarkable isn't usually directly related to the original purpose of the product or service. It's the extra stuff, the stylish bonus, the design or the remarkable service or pricing that makes people talk about it and spread the word."

\- Seth Godin

The origin of the goldfish dates back to 2009. It represents something small, but despite its size, something with the ability to make a big difference.

The first part of the inspiration for the goldfish came from Kimpton Hotels. The boutique hotel chain introduced something new in 2001. The Kimpton Hotel Monaco began to offer travelers the opportunity to adopt a temporary travel companion for their stay. Perhaps you are traveling on business and getting a little lonely. Or maybe you are with family and missing your family pet. Kimpton to the rescue; they will give you a goldfish for your stay. They called the program Guppy Love.

> "The 'Guppy Love' program is a fun extension of our pet-friendly nature as well as our emphasis on indulging the senses to heighten the travel experience," says Steve Pinetti, Senior Vice President of Sales & Marketing for Kimpton Hotels and Restaurants. "Everything about Kimpton Hotel Monaco appeals directly to the senses, and 'Guppy Love' offers one more unique way to relax, indulge and promote health of mind, body and spirit in our home-away-from-home atmosphere."

The second part of our goldfish inspiration came from the peculiar growth of a goldfish. The average common goldfish is between three to four inches in length (ten centimeters), yet the largest in the world is almost six times that size! For comparison, imagine walking down the street and bumping into someone who's three stories tall.

How can there be such a disparity between regular goldfish and their monster cousins? Well, it turns out that the growth of the goldfish is determined by five factors. Just like goldfish, not all businesses grow equally and we believe that the growth of a product or service faces the same five factors that affect the growth of a goldfish.

#1. SIZE OF THE ENVIRONMENT = THE MARKET

Growth Factor: The size of the bowl or pond.

Impact: Direct correlation. The larger the bowl or pond, the larger the goldfish can grow. Similarly, the smaller the market in business, the lesser the growth potential.

#2. NUMBER OF OTHER GOLDFISH IN THE BOWL OR POND = COMPETITION

Growth Factor: The number of goldfish in the same bowl or pond.

Impact: Inverse correlation. The more goldfish, the less growth. Similarly, the less competition in business, the more growth opportunity exists.

#3. THE QUALITY OF THE WATER = THE ECONOMY

Growth Factor: The clarity and amount of nutrients in the water.

Impact: Direct correlation. The better the quality, the larger the growth. Similarly, the weaker the economy or capital markets in business, the more difficult it is too grow.

FACT

A malnourished goldfish in a crowded, cloudy environment may only grow to two inches (five centimeters).

#4. THE FIRST 120 DAYS OF LIFE = STARTUP PHASE OR A NEW PRODUCT LAUNCH

Growth Factor: The nourishment and treatment received as a fry (baby goldfish).

Impact: Direct correlation. The lower the quality of the food, water, and treatment, the more the goldfish will be stunted for future growth. Similarly, in business, the stronger the leadership and capital for a start-up, the better the growth.

#5. GENETIC MAKEUP = DIFFERENTIATION

Growth Factor: The genetic makeup of the goldfish.

Impact: Direct correlation. The poorer the genes or the less differentiated, the less the goldfish can grow. Similarly, in business, the more differentiated the product or service from the competition, the better the chance for growth.

FACT

The current *Guinness Book of World Records* holder for the largest goldfish hails from The Netherlands at a whopping 19 inches (50 centimeters). To put that in perspective, that's about the size of the average domestic cat.

WHICH OF THE FIVE FACTORS CAN YOU CONTROL?

Let's assume you have an existing product or service and have been in business for more than four months. Do you have any control over the market, your competition, or the economy? NO, NO, and NO.

The only thing you have control over is your business's genetic makeup or how you differentiate your product or service. For franchises, that's the experience you provide to franchisees and customers. In goldfish terms, how do you stand out in a sea of sameness?

Now, why the color purple?

CHAPTER 3

WHY PURPLE?

"We picked up one excellent word—
a word worth traveling to New Orleans to get;
a nice limber, expressive, handy word—lagniappe"

- Mark Twain

The reasons for choosing the color purple are two-fold:

#1. MARDI GRAS

Purple is an ode to the birthplace of the word, New Orleans, and the colors of its most famous event, Mardi Gras.

The most commonly held story behind the original selection of the Mardi Gras colors originates from 1872 when the Grand Duke of Russia, Alexei Romanov, visited New Orleans. Legend has it that the Grand Duke came to New Orleans in pursuit of a British actress named Lydia Thompson, and during his stay, Romanov was given the honor of selecting the official Mardi Gras colors by the Krewe of Rex. His selection of purple, green, and gold would also later become the colors of the House of Romanov.

The 1892 "Rex Parade" theme first gave meaning to the official Mardi Gras colors. Inspired by New Orleans and its traditional colors, purple was symbolic of justice, green was symbolic of faith, and gold was symbolic of power. The first three books in the Goldfish series were *Purple Goldfish, Green Goldfish,* and *Golden Goldfish.*

#2. ODE TO SETH

Purple in marketing represents differentiation. Seth Godin established purple as the color of differentiation in his seminal book, *Purple Cow,* back in 2003. Seth outlines the why, what, and how of becoming remarkable.

Seth sets up the premise of the book with a story:

> When my family and I were driving through France a few years ago, we were enchanted by the hundreds of storybook cows grazing on picturesque pastures right

> next to the highway. For dozens of kilometers, we all gazed out the window, marveling about how beautiful everything was. Then, within twenty minutes, we started ignoring the cows. The new cows were just like the old cows, and what was once amazing was now common. Worse than common. It was boring.

Seth went further and defined where marketing is heading by saying, "The old rule: Create safe, ordinary products and combine them with great marketing. The new rule: Create remarkable products that the right people seek out."

PURPLE BOVINE VS. PURPLE GOLDFISH

Think of a "Purple Cow" as your product. Your product needs to stand out and be remarkable. A Purple Goldfish, on the other hand, is the distinctive way that you deliver that purple cow and the extra value that you provide. It's difficult to make a product stand out by itself, but there is low hanging fruit in adding value to your offering.

The difficulty in Seth Godin's "Purple Cow" principle is that you need to bake that remarkability into the product. That is extremely difficult to accomplish. But what if you created a few Purple Goldfish instead? A goldfish is something a whole lot smaller than a cow and much easier to create. Can small "purple" things make a big difference? Absolutely.

Imagine if you asked a friend for a recommendation and they started gushing about "Product X" because of signature experience. It could be the customer service they received that they were not expecting (think: ChickfilA), a feature that the company decided not to charge for (think: Southwest and "Bags Fly Free"), or a small "thank you" gift with your purchase (think: Five Guys Burgers).

TURNING A PURPLE GOLDFISH INTO STRATEGY

The Purple Goldfish strategy advocates differentiation by adding value to the end consumers. This encompasses (1) finding signature elements that help you stand out, (2) improving customer experience, (3) reducing attrition and (4) driving positive word of mouth. This makes the customer experience more important than ever, and there are three leading indicators.

First, the cost of customer acquisition continues to rise, making increasing retention the lowest hanging fruit in marketing. Second, consumers now have a stronger voice given the emergence of social technologies like blogs, Facebook, YouTube, Instagram, Snapchat, TripAdvisor, and Yelp. Finally, competing solely on price will "commoditize" your product or service faster than ever.

A SIMPLE MARKETING CONCEPT

Is it possible to move the needle toward achieving differentiation while driving retention and stimulating word of mouth? What if your marketing execution was 100% targeted with zero waste and was given with a personalized touch? It sounds like a fantasy, but we promise you that it's not.

We believe the answer lies in focusing a greater percentage of your marketing budget on your current franchisees and customers rather than your prospects. Put another way, allocating your attention to the "one in hand" rather than the "two in the bush" through a concept called, "lagniappe."

WHAT IS LAGNIAPPE?

Lagniappe is a Creole word meaning "the gift" or "to give more." The practice originated in Louisiana in the 1840's where a merchant would give a customer a little something extra at the time of their purchase. It is a signature personal touch by the business that creates goodwill and promotes word of mouth. According to Merriam Webster:

LAGNIAPPE: (lan'yəəp, lăn-yăp') *Chiefly Southern Louisiana & Mississippi*

1. A small gift presented by a store owner to a customer with their purchase.
2. An extra or unexpected gift or benefit. Also called boot.

Etymology: Creole < Fr la, the + Sp ñapa, lagniappe < Quechuan yapa

ENTER SAMUEL LANGHORNE CLEMENS

Mark Twain was smitten with the concept of lagniappe. He wrote about the concept in his memoir, *Life on the Mississippi*:

> We picked up one excellent word—a word worth traveling to New Orleans to get; a nice limber, expressive, handy word—"lagniappe." They pronounce it lanny-yap. It is Spanish- so they said. We discovered it at the head of a column of odds and ends in the [Times] Picayune [newspaper] the first day; heard twenty people use it the second; inquired what it meant the third; adopted it and got facility in swinging it the fourth. It has a restricted meaning, but I think the people spread it out a little when they choose. It is the equivalent of the thirteenth roll in a baker's dozen. It is something thrown in, gratis, for good measure. The custom originated in the Spanish quarter of the city. When a child or a servant buys something in a shop—or even the mayor or the governor, for aught I know—he finishes the operation by saying—'Give me something for

> lagniappe.' The shopman always responds; gives the child a bit of licoriceroot, gives the servant a cheap cigar or a spool of thread, gives the governor—I don't know what he gives the governor; support, likely.

A lagniappe, a Purple Goldfish, is any time a business purposely goes above and beyond to provide a little something extra. It's a marketing investment back into your customer base. It's that unexpected surprise that's thrown in for good measure to achieve product differentiation, drive retention, and promote word of mouth.

IS IT JUST A BAKER'S DOZEN?

Some people assert that lagniappe is merely the baker's dozen but it most certainly isn't. In order to understand a baker's dozen, we need to travel back to its origin in England. The concept dates back to the 13th century during the reign of Henry III[6].

During this time, there was a perceived need for regulations controlling quality, pricing, and checking weights to avoid fraudulent activity in the baking industry. The Assize (Statute) of Bread and Ale was instituted to regulate the price, weight, and quality of the bread and beer manufactured and sold in towns, villages, and hamlets.

Bakers who were found to have shortchanged customers could be liable for severe punishment such as losing a hand via an axe. To guard against the punishment, the baker would give 13 for the price of 12, to be certain of not being known as a cheat (and subsequently to keep their hand). The irony is that the statute deals with weight and not the quantity. The merchants created the "baker's dozen" to change perception. They understood that one of the 13 could be

6. http://mentalfloss.com/article/32259/whybakersdozen13

lost, eaten, burnt, or ruined in some way, leaving the customer with the original legal dozen.

Flash forward to centuries later and a baker's dozen has now become expected. Nowadays when we walk into a bakery and buy a dozen bagels, we expect the thirteenth on the house. Therefore, the baker's dozen is not a lagniappe. However, if you provided a fourteenth bagel as part of the dozen then that would be a Purple Goldfish.

ACTS OF KINDNESS

Another way to think of lagniappe is as an act of kindness. We have identified three "Acts of Kindness" to distinguish exactly what we mean:

1. **Random Act of Kindness** – "1.0" version. We've all seen this before. Good deeds or unexpected acts such as upgrading a passenger to first class on a flight or offering a free dessert for consumers. They are usually one-off, feelgood activities. A random act of kindness draws upon gift economy principles in that they are given with no expectation of immediate return except for potential PR value.

2. **Branded Act of Kindness** – Next level or "2.0." Here the item given is usually tied closely with the brand and its positioning. It's less random, more planned, and involves a series of events. This has the feel of a traditional marketing campaign and many brands are moving in this direction. According to the former EVP/CMO of CocaCola Joe Tripodi, "Coke is leaning more toward 'expressions' than traditional 'impressions.'" In other words, less eyeballs and more emphasis on touches. What is an expression or a touch? It's a like on Facebook, a video on YouTube, sharing a photo of your product, a tweet on Twitter, and so forth.

3. Lagniappe Act of Kindness – "3.0" level acts are manifested through kindness being embedded into the brand. Giving little unexpected extras (G.L.U.E.) as part of your product or service. This is rooted in the idea of added value to every single transaction. Not a one-off or a campaign, but an everyday practice that's focused on customers of your brand. The beauty of creating this type of Purple Goldfish is that there is no waste. You are giving that little extra to your current customers and accounting for it.

PLUSSING: THE IMPORTANCE OF EXCEEDING EXPECTATIONS

When talking about exceeding expectations, an entire book could be written about Walt Disney and the principles that make Disney a magical place. In fact, Pat Williams did just that and penned an incredible book called, *How to Be Like Walt: Capturing the Disney Magic Every Day of Your Life*[7]. The book talks about a concept Walt called plussing:

Normally, the word 'plus' is a conjunction, but not in Walt's vocabulary. To Walt, 'plus' was a verb—an action word—signifying the delivery of more than what his customers paid for or expected to receive.

There are literally hundreds, if not thousands, of examples of Walt "plussing" his products. He constantly challenged his artists and Imagineers to see what was possible and then take it a step further... and then a step beyond that. Why did he go to the trouble of making everything better when "good enough" would have sufficed? Because for Walt, nothing less than the best was acceptable when it bore his name and reputation, and he did whatever it took to give his guests more value than they expected to receive for their dollar.

---

7. ttp://www.amazon.com/HowBeLikeWaltCapturing/dp/0757302319

Perhaps one of the best examples of Walt's obsession for "plussing" comes from Disney historian Les Perkins' account of an incident that took place at Disneyland during the early years of the park. Walt had decided to hold a Christmas parade at the new park at a cost of $350,000. Walt's accountants approached him and besieged him to not spend money on an extravagant Christmas parade because the people would already be there. Nobody would complain, they reasoned, if they dispensed with the parade because nobody would be expecting it. Walt's reply to his accountants is classic: "That's just the point," he said. "We should do the parade precisely because no one's expecting it. Our goal at Disneyland is to always give the people more than they expect. As long as we keep surprising them, they'll keep coming back. But if they ever stop coming, it'll cost us ten times that much to get them to come back."

PART II

KEYS TO FRANCHISING

CHAPTER 4

DEVELOPING A S.Y.S.T.E.M.

"Everything must be made as simple as possible. But not simpler."

— Albert Einstein

WHY A S.Y.S.T.E.M?

Prospective franchisees and new franchisees in training are bombarded with the advice to "follow the system." Experienced franchisees and the franchisor will continuously talk about the "system." When franchise rights are granted, utilization of the attending "system" remains one of the biggest of benefits of signing the Franchise Agreement. As Bob Gappa, CEO and founder of Management 2000 and a franchise expert, shares, "Franchising is a strategy that a company uses to create and keep very satisfied and loyal customers, who continue to use its products and services and who recommend it to others." Bob continues with additional benefits to franchising for both the franchisor and franchisee, yet this first statement points to the "system" of creating customer value that generates benefits for the customer, the franchisee, and the franchisor.

As we explore each area of the franchise SYSTEM, keep in mind why franchisors exist and let that become a lens that focuses the franchisor on what is important. Franchisees choose franchises for a safety net- an operating SYSTEM. According to the Small Business Administration, about one-third of small businesses will fail in the first two years. About half fail in the first five years and two-thirds will close their doors by year ten.[8] Forty- two percent of small businesses fail because there is no need for their product, while 19% fail because their competition out maneuvered them and another 17% fail because they do not have a profitable model.[9]

Franchise SYSTEMS overcome these reasons for failure. As Bob Gappa describes franchising, the franchisee is singing a song they did not write. It was created by someone else. The song already has a melody, words, emotion, etc., yet the franchisee will add customer value by putting their emotion into their rendition of the song.

---

8. https://www.fundera.com/blog/what-percentage-of-small-businesses-fail
9. https://www.fundera.com/blog/what-percentage-of-small-businesses-fail

They hope their audience will want them to sing for them again, and again – they want to create encore experiences for their audience. In this case, the song is the ways the franchisee injects his/her self into the implementation of the franchised business model while they deliver its products and/or services to the customers. The most successful singers want to create strong emotional connections with their audiences. Similarly, the most successful franchisees will create an emotional connection within their customers to the franchised Brand they are representing. This process makes customers return to franchised locations just like it makes fans return to a singer or a bands concerts.

As Gappa additionally explains, it is the emotions that create the lasting bond between a brand and its customers. The customers give the franchised business locations financial currency in exchange for an experience involving goods and services. The franchisee of the Brand, in return, gives the customers emotional currency. The emotional currency is what makes the customers WANT to return. So what used to be called "Economics" is now called "Emotionomics." This emotional connection lies in the heart of Purple Goldfish Franchise Edition. The franchisor focuses on creating, delivering and maintaining a SYSTEM that the franchisee embraces and executes with passion. When the SYSTEM is delivered mechanically it is known as a transaction. When it is delivered with personal commitment it is known as an experience. That passion tethers the SYSTEM together and makes the customer WANT to return again and again. It boils down to management of expectations. The SYSTEM's processes, technologies, and human elements together manage customers' expectations and builds life-long, loyal customers and brand advocates.

The difference between 20th and 21st century franchising, according to Gappa, is that in the 20th century a franchisee was "in business for myself but not by myself" while in the 21st century I am "in business with the franchisor, and my fellow franchisees, working collaboratively, to build a Brand where customers WANT to come to spend money because the feel happy before during and after their experiences with the Brand's experiences created by the franchisees and their teams. In the 20th century, the franchisee was a customer, but now in the 21st century, the franchisee is a Strategic-Partner in creating the growth of their Brand.

Often, franchisees will ask what the system entails and receive nebulous answers that focus on Franchise Agreement requirements and recommended/required marketing tools and practices. Yet the "system" boils down to key franchisor areas that, when executed well and in sync with one another, optimize franchisee opportunity and thus franchisor performance. The S.Y.S.T.E.M. entails: Selection, Yield, Start Up, Training, Engagement and Culture, and Manage.

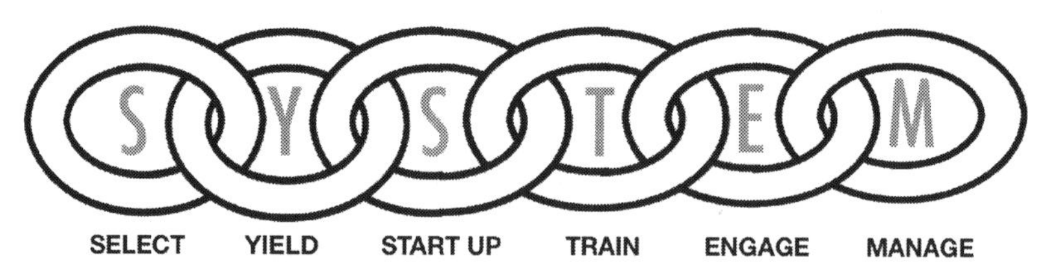

Within the SYSTEM, each piece links together, and it is the sum of adding each piece that makes the total worth more. Selecting the right people makes everything easier and preserves the culture. Yielding harnesses the knowledge of the franchisor and puts it to work to fulfill the reason or the why behind a person's choice to join a franchise. Starting on the right foot accelerates success while training takes that success to a new level systemwide. Starting with the right people makes it easier to maintain the culture and cultivate engagement as the SYSTEM holds true to the promise made at the time of signing the Franchise Agreement. Manage is living up to the culture and delivering the intended customer experience to delight the customer and have them return frequently. Manage is also delivering the right experience to delight and support your franchisees.

Each piece in this chain is important. While it is possible for each piece to stand on its own, an optimized well performing SYSTEM must execute each piece well. A weak link can cause vulnerability. Keeping each link in the SYSTEM strong codifies forming a strong bond that propels success. It's the strength of each piece that makes the total body of the SYSTEM stronger, better able to withstand challenges, more adaptive to opportunity, and better able to fulfill the why behind the reason that each franchisee signed on.

Just as a body is made of many parts that function together as one unit, each piece of the six-part S.Y.S.T.E.M. has its own function and importance, and each supports the others to create the whole. The following sections examine each piece of this chain.

1. SELECTION

Choosing the right franchisee is akin to building a solid foundation. You cannot train what you don't have, so choose wisely. Franchisees are the life blood of the organization. They add new ideas, become brand ambassadors, and provide customer touch points faster than the franchisor can pace. Consider the benefits that a great franchisee can bring to the franchise S.Y.S.T.E.M. and remember well the repercussions of unsuitable franchisee/franchisor relationships (think franchisee lawsuit disclosures in Franchise Disclosure Documents), and you have significant reasons to select wisely.
The franchisee must have the ability to deliver an emotional connection to the target customer in order to achieve repeat business. This is the opportunity to add that right person to the mix.

According to an *Entrepreneur* article[10] by Mark Siebert, Franchise Consultant for Start-Up and Established Franchisors:

10. https://www.entrepreneur.com/article/72802

> In order to assess these soft criteria, franchisors are increasingly using more sophisticated assessment tools to "benchmark" the "job" of their franchisees. These tools are then used by franchisees to determine their compatibility for the role. But regardless of whether or not you use these tools, assessing the job of the franchisee—and ultimately doing what you can to assure the franchisee's success—is the most important and most difficult job of every franchisor.

Once selected, the newly minted franchisee must successfully move through the other pieces of the SYSTEM links. Yield is the next link that we discuss.

2. YIELD

Yield includes two pieces. One piece deals with Knowledge of the franchisor plus the collective franchisee base. The other piece of this link involves Comply and Produce, the act of following and benefiting from the Knowledge of the franchisor and franchisee base. This includes complying with the requirements of the franchisor in order to produce the desired results. The franchisee has many obligations to the franchisor. Franchise Agreements contain numerous sections filled with requirements of the franchisees. The agreement is a license granted for benefit and gain by both parties, the franchisee and franchisor. Some franchisors seem requirement happy, listing a laundry list of requirements that at the end of the day, do not move the needle. To illustrate this point, Bob Gappa provides an example - the bathrooms must be clean at all times. In this example, clean bathrooms is the standard. The standard does not tell you how to achieve the standard. So the franchisor gives the franchisee best practices to achieve the standard, but the best practices are not the standard itself. In this example, is it important how many ounces of cleaner are used per cleaning, or is it important that the bathrooms are clean? This takes us to the focal point of Yield- use knowledge to create requirements, standards. Help franchisees comply with best practices and measure what they produce, the items that actually produce an experience that customers engages customers, delights customers and makes the customer choose your brand again and again.

In an *Entrepreneur* article[11], "Four Mistakes that Will Sink Your Franchise Dream," author Aaron Bakke, a franchise owner, warns, "Remember: You're part of a franchise group. The worst mistake a new franchise owner can make is ignoring the proven procedures outlined by the franchise. If you don't take program and processes seriously, you'll greatly limit your chances for success."

Franchisors can increase the likelihood of a franchisee following the system with best practices. For example, according to Keith Gerson, CEO of FranConnect, the Dwyer Group has a few rules, and they talk about them all of the time to make sure franchisees focus on what drives success. So, keep the SYSTEM alive by sharing Knowledge and make it simpler to Comply and Produce results.

3. START UP

Start Up procedures lead to success early in the franchisee's life cycle. The stronger the start, the more likely the franchisee will achieve their goals, expand, and validate the concept well. Often, new franchisees feel like they are drowning as start-up training and procedures flow faster than water from a firehose. The franchisor must break the training and procedures into manageable chunks so that the new franchisee can move through each step systematically without becoming paralyzed by the overwhelming nature of starting a business.

11. https://www.entrepreneur.com/article/312475

Some franchisors excel with pairing resources to make Start Up more palatable and fast track the franchisee through to performing. With onboarding costs sometimes equaling the initial territory fee, franchisors should have a strong incentive to fast track sustainable franchisee success.

4. TRAINING

Continuous Training will positively impact several parts of the SYSTEM including Engagement and Culture as well as lead to understanding the Key Performance Indicators that drive the business and Yield results. For most franchises, ongoing training is one of the key benefits of becoming a franchisee rather than going it alone and having to learn and do everything yourself. Some franchisors view this as so important that they use creative tools and methods to continually improve their franchise base, which in turn drives unit growth and expansion for them.

5. ENGAGEMENT AND CULTURE

Engagement shines brightly in franchises that cultivate Culture. According to the International Franchise Association:

> In many ways, franchise organizations are even more dependent upon a positive culture than other business models. The franchisee group is composed of independent business owners, often with entrepreneurial spirit, and less inclined to follow instructions than typical employees and managers. They, and their employee teams, must be persuaded to conform to the franchise model because it's the right thing to do for the underlying brand and benefits the franchisee. A strong, positive culture with a commitment from the entire franchise organization will make franchise

> model compliance more likely, and enhance the entire franchise group[12].

Unlike financial performance, which is measured and reviewed regularly and is considered a key to success, culture is rarely measured and effectively viewed. A deeper look may identify a company's culture as its biggest asset or greatest liability.

In many ways, franchise organizations are even more dependent upon a positive culture than other business models. The franchisee group is composed of independent business owners, often with entrepreneurial spirit, and therefore less inclined to follow instructions than typical employees and managers. They, and their employee teams, must be persuaded to conform to the franchise model because it's the right thing to do for the underlying brand and benefits the franchisee.

For some franchisors, Engagement and Culture is amplified through the execution of well selected and trained franchisees. As Whitney Preslar shared in a post about Chick-fil-A, "Whichever store you visit, the store is just a little brighter and the smiles a little wider than other places. And when a new store opens, customers will line up for a chance to win free food from the chain. Sometimes a smile makes food taste better!" This is an example where the franchisor culture is consistently clear and franchisees engage to consistently deliver the intended experience every time. In these cases, Engagement is best visible through the franchisee amplification of the franchisor Culture.

6. MANAGE

Manage has two pieces. One part involves Support or in other words, the structure that a franchisor uses to aid the franchisee's

12. https://www.franchise.org/creating-a-positive-franchise-culture

success. The other part involves Advertising, the customer acquisition model and associated tools that produce customers, as well as customer experience, retention, and hopefully delight.

As for Support, the International Franchise Association lists five keys to franchisor support:

1. Regionalized Support
2. Broadcast on Channel WII-FM (What's In It For Me) aka the franchisee
3. Correct Allocation of Time
4. Get in the Trenches
5. Live by the Numbers[13]

Franchise support requires a delicate balance between entrepreneurship with buy-in and acceptance of the franchise SYSTEM. Trust between the franchisor and franchisee as business partners is vital in this combination of my-way entrepreneurial drive and the power of the franchise knowledge, experience, and culture that can be (must be) claimed through the SYSTEM. Personal goals drive business goals, so when the two goals align, magic happens. To make the magic, the support person must have a relations where the franchisee feels comfortable and wants to share personal goals.

With Advertising, franchisees benefit from consolidated advertising purchases and the power of professionally crafted marketing tools. The franchisor benefits from the broader spend that franchisees invest, often adding marketing spend that the franchisor would not have alone. And amazingly, some franchisors channel that spend to deliver 80 percent of the franchisee's customer base.

13. https://www.franchise.org/five-must-do-franchise-support-tactics

Regardless of your industry, make no mistake, successful franchises are in the customer delight business. Customer "delightment" always a business to acquire customers and retain them. Peter Drucker in his book *The Five Most Important Questions You Will Ever Ask About Your Organization* proposes five questions with regard to business success and the questions apply very much to how franchisor-provided advertising tools work within a SYSTEM:

1. What is your mission?

2. Who is your customer?

3. What does your customer value?

4. What are your results?

5. What is your plan?

This leads to the advertising part of Manage - create customers, retain and build frequency.

To the job of the franchisor with advertising, Bob Gappa shares that in the 21st Century, people who love you make you a brand. People who like what you do, make you well known; there are many well-known companies but few are loved. Why do we love companies? It is emotional, it is how the customer feels before, during and after doing business with you. And that is a sum of your SYSTEM and the franchisee execution SYSTEM by infusion passion to execute on point marketing and customer experience tools. Emotion breeds loyalty. To quote Gappa:

> These feelings are like currency, 'emotional currency'. This is the moment where everything changes, the paradigm of business shifts.We are no longer exchanging our goods and services for the financial currency of the customer. We are exchanging the ways we feel

> about the customer [most have already decided to buy our goods and services], our 'emotional currency' for their 'financial currency'. This 'currency exchange' is the essence and core of understanding the new 'experience economy' we are living and working in at this very moment.

Gappa adds that brands market emotions that they know that you the customer want to feel. The three top emotions for building connections include Happy, Belonging, and Comfortable. So, it is no mistake that McDonald's offers a Happy Meal, or that Starbucks wants customers to feel comfortable. Imbedding emotion in to your SYSTEM and selecting franchisee who exhibit passion stretch advertising miles!

The next six chapters will explore each element of the S.Y.S.T.E.M. in greater detail and provide best of breed examples for each.

CHAPTER 5

SELECTION

"Great vision without great people is irrelevant"

-Jim Collins, *Good to Great*

Selection is akin to starting off on the right foot. Most franchisors have learned the hard way that you cannot fix what you miss. And a franchisee not aligned to the values and mission of the franchisor will potentially lead not only to lost opportunity but also to the possibility of a poisoned well for others. This miss is a poor validation for future prospects. At minimum, the mis-matched franchisee will likely sit in a territory underperforming, thus maximizing neither the franchisee nor franchisor return on investment while potentially providing the franchise with a poor reputation in the marketplace as well as with other franchisees.

Referring to such cases, Greg Nathan, Managing Director of the Franchisee Relationships Institute states that "...there is the loss of royalty revenues and local damage to the brand. These costs will typically add up to $250,000 for a retail franchise and can be in the tens of thousands of dollars for a service-based franchise. But there are also the indirect costs to a franchise system associated with the negative attitudes typically associated with franchisee failure[14]."

Not everyone is cut out to fulfill the franchisee role—that perfect balance of entrepreneur mixed with SYSTEM follower and team player who can perform individually at their franchise level. Yet sometimes the selection process feels like you are a contestant on the TV show *The Bachelor*; speed dating that quickly leads to a proposal. And let's face it, the franchisee to franchisor relationship is a long-term commitment where both parties need to fit, similar to a marriage!

To further illustrate the point of Selection, Nathan states:

> Assuming that a franchise system is based on a proven business concept with sound training and support sys-

---

14. http://www.franchiserelationships.com/articles/BestPracticesinFranchiseeEvaluation.html

> tems, we estimate that around 40% of a franchisee's success will come through the application of their own hard work and talents. This is a significant amount, and a franchisee who does not have the attributes for success is likely to fail. Unfortunately, the rigorous screening of franchisees for these attributes is the exception rather than the rule[15].

In some cases, the thrill of a new prospect, especially for young startups, fuels the heartbeat like a speed date with an attractive person. But how many times have you dated someone only to find that what looks like the power of a Ferrari on the outside has a tiny 4-cylinder motor on the inside? And just as you do not want to commit to a lifetime with a hollow person, you do not want to sign a franchise agreement with a mis-matched franchisee. Proper selection remains paramount to kickstart a new venture, to fuel a mature one, and to ensure continued growth.

Some franchisors utilize different approaches to ensure that the franchisee fits. The next 11 examples showcase franchise systems that have some novel approaches to ensure that the franchisee is a fit to fuel your SYSTEM.

1. CertaPro makes Certa of fit -- Former Franchisee Tim Johnson shares the impressive steps taken to ensure a proper franchise fit as he explores the CertaPro franchise opportunity. Tim shares that CertaPro uses a Discovery Day, where along the way, prospects will "jump through the hoop" to show their serious desire to become a franchisee. The franchisor also uses personality and problem-solving tests to learn more about the candidate. The results are calibrated to top performers to determine the ideal franchisee candidate.

---

15. http://www.franchiserelationships.com/articles/BestPracticesinFranchiseeEvaluation.html

2. Dream Vacations deal franchise dreams -- Want to buy a franchise? Well, Dream Vacations isn't selling franchises. They are selling dreams! In an interview in Travel Pulse, Dream Vacation's Senior VP Debbie Fiorina shared, "We don't sell franchises, we award dream businesses to people who are passionate about travel and helping others.[16]" In this case, understand what type of franchisee you seek as a franchisor, discern the slight degrees of difference that leave someone aligned with your culture vs. not aligned, and remain selective with whom you invite to partner.

3. Sail with me -- Founder and CEO Debi Lane of Lunchboxwax, a full-service body waxing salon franchise, has a clear vision about what she seeks in a franchisee. In a recent franchising article in *Southwest Airlines Magazine,* Lane stated that she "...asks herself each time: Could I spend a fulfilling and enjoyable week on a sailboat with this person?" While not her only criterion, it demonstrates the franchisor's commitment to only selecting those who fit with the culture. Lane adds, "We're redefining what success means in business by placing priority on fostering each person's EQ or emotional intelligence as well as their ability to run and grow a business.[17]"

4. BUZZ with the mission -- Selecting franchisees who align with the franchise mission adds many benefits. Buzz Franchise Brands—Mosquito Joe, Pool Scout, and Home Clean Heros—uses a straightforward approach of sharing the mission with prospects at the very beginning. During Decision Day, Mosquito Joe sees sharing the mission as a key strategy to success. Prospects must know about mission and values to give them a sense of who it is they would be joining should they become franchisees.[18]

---

16. https://www.travelpulse.com/news/host-agency-and-consortia/dream-vacations-earns-high-marks-among-franchise-owners.html
17. https://issuu.com/southwestmag/docs/july2018/14,
18. http://go.franconnect.com/webinar-ceo-secrets-watch-now?submissionGuid=beddcfab-635c-46c9-8c61-33f973d9fa81

5. Jimmy John's franchise prospect menu -- Jimmy John's prospect selection comes right off the menu with straightforward communication. Toasted up right on their website, Jimmy John's lets prospects know from the start what they seek. Those without the right ingredients need not apply. From their website:

> **Who We Let Do This Deal**
>
> Think you have what it takes?
>
> 1. You have to have the cash.
>
> 2. Real passion for my brand. If you don't dig it as much as we all dig it, this brand is not for you!
>
> 3. You've got to be a good, hard-working, well-intentioned individual, who respects yourself and others.
>
> 4. You've got to be disciplined and able to take specific, detailed direction extremely well.
>
> 5. You can't be a criminal.
>
> 6. You've got to love life, kids, music, dancing, your grandparents, and sandwiches.
>
> 7. Lastly, you've got to be excited to work harder than you ever have in your entire life[19].

6. Decked up for success with Deka -- Following a system is key to...well, following a franchise SYSTEM. To learn if a prospect is serious about Deka Lash, Michael Debenham, COO, says that the franchisor provides homework to prospects. Their timely completion and effort show how serious the prospect is about owning a franchise. And if a prospect can follow Deka's process of timely

---

19. https://www.jimmyjohns.com/franchising/who-we-let-do-this-deal/

assignment completion while showing effort, then Deka is more comfortable that the franchisee will follow the franchise SYSTEM.

7. **Ordering up a great franchisee** -- Similarly, Order Up wants to test a potential franchisee's ability to follow their SYSTEM because what is the point of a SYSTEM if it is not followed?

As part of the process, prospective franchisees are sent to their desired market to complete assignments. The assignment usually includes looking around the area for potential business opportunities and completing a prescribed development plan. However, the point of the assignment is to discern if the franchisee can follow instructions, an indicator if they are likely to follow a SYSTEM and to look at the effort applied as a proxy to indicate the prospect's interest in joining Order Up. The more effort reflected, the more likely it seems the prospect will follow their SYSTEM. Order Up understands that the actions of a prospective franchisee speak louder than words.

According to Mark Johnson, CEO of Franchise This, homework tests serve as an indicator of success, but are not necessarily 100 percent predictive. This may just indicate book smarts versus determination to carry out and follow the SYSTEM over time. Johnson offers that it seems the more expensive the franchise, the more predictive testing the franchisor uses, including even health testing, because the investment is significant for both franchisees and franchisor.

8. **Dutch Bros. gives loyalty to the Bros.** -- Sometimes, looking within provides the best source of growth. Someone who has spent years learning and contributing to the mission not only knows how to operate a successful location but also knows what they are signing up to do. According to a recent Forbes online article by Forbes Staff Susan Adams:

> Aiming to speed expansion, Dutch Bros. started offering extraordinarily generous terms to loyal employees like Kristen Von Tersch, who started as a minimum-wage bro-ista when she was nineteen. To buy her five franchises, she had to put up only $5,000. By contrast, Dunkin' Donuts requires franchisees to have liquid assets of at least $250,000 and a net worth of $500,000 per store. To cover the rest of Kristen's investment, including the $30,000-per-store franchise fee plus depreciated equipment costs, Dutch Bros. loaned her $250,000 at 12% interest, amortized over ten years. She pays rent on the real estate and a royalty of 7% of her gross.[20]

9. No monkeying around at clothier Monkee's -- Monkee's, a women's clothing and gift shop, is focused on service and doesn't monkey around when selecting franchisees. While most franchisors have a prospect trek to their corporate office for a discovery day, Monkee's comes to the prospect's market. From the franchisor's website, Monkee's shares that "We will meet you in your market and spend most of the day getting to know you, answering more questions and touring potential locations for your Monkee's store.[21]"

10. Right at Home selects franchisees who feel right at home -- According to the *PR Newswire* article:

> Right at Home looks for franchisees who naturally demonstrate a compassion to care for others. If you were looking for someone to care for you or a loved one, naturally you would select someone who enjoys helping others. Right at Home's philosophy permeates

20. https://www.forbes.com/sites/susanadams/2016/06/15/the-coffee-cult-how-dutch-bros-is-turning-its-bro-istas-into-wealthy-franchisees/#6d92832a3694
21. http://www.shopmonkees.com/ownership/our-selection-process/

> their SYSTEM to deliver the intended customer experience. In the release, Brian Petranick, Right at Home CEO and President, shares, "From our caregivers to our franchise owners to our corporate staff, Right at Home fosters a culture that cares. We are committed to providing a holistic, individualized RightCare experience for every client to improve their quality of life...[22]

11. It takes a coffee filter -- Does your franchise have a no-jerks filter? At Maui Wowi hiring and franchisee selection have a culture fit test to ensure the right blend. In an *Entrepreneur* online article by contributor Jason Daly, Maui Wowi looks for those who fit with ohana, conveying the concept and culture of family in the Hawaiian language[23].

In that article, CEO Mike Weinberger shares that "Cultural fit is so important to Maui Wowi that each prospective corporate employee is interviewed by the entire staff, from the office manager on up.... One person can make a toxic atmosphere. [Prospects] have to have the right mindset and fit in well. Our staff filters out the jerks."

And he lets his franchisees do the same, vetting candidates before they can attend Discovery Day, rejecting those who don't seem like they would fit in the family.

CHAPTER RECAP: SELECTION

Selecting the right people is an investment in an annuity that generates continual growth both in terms of the SYSTEM and the unit level profitability. As the saying goes, an ounce of prevention is

22. https://www.prnewswire.com/news-releases/right-at-home-named-no-1-franchise-opportunity-under-150-000-by-forbes-magazine-300672918.html,
23. https://www.entrepreneur.com/article/253840

better than a pound of cure. Plus, the right people make the rest of the SYSTEM much easier and smoother.

CHAPTER 6

YIELD

"Our chief want in life is somebody who will make us do what we can."

— Ralph Waldo Emerson

A primary benefit of a franchise is the SYSTEM. Starting a business, you will either pay tuition to the school of life or you will pay royalties. Many find that the royalty route is one that brings the fastest route to success. And here lies the tricky part of a franchise—the balance of being able to follow a system and having an owner's drive to succeed in the face of challenge. So, this section houses examples regarding **Yield**. Yield entails yielding to the **Knowledge** in the franchisor's system *along with* the ability to **Comply** and **Produce** within the SYSTEM.

Knowledge - Franchisors possess the Knowledge to fast track a business. This knowledge comes from various sources, including past experience and trial and error as well as learning from top performers. Some franchisors possess unique ways to harvest and deploy this key element.

Applied Knowledge - McDonald's is the king of franchising, so let's take a look at what McDonald's promises franchisees. Simply, it is a SYSTEM! After years of leading the franchise space, McDonald's has perfected implementation to minimize tuition to the school of life.

From a Wealth Management article written by Michael Thrasher, investment advisor Brad Griswold, the managing partner of Corbenic Partners in Bethlehem, Pennsylvania, shared an example about McDonald's breakfast implementation and the attention to detail that knowledge brings, used in making even the smallest decision:

> Griswold said one benefit of McDonald's franchises is the organizational and capital support from the parent company, which not all owners of franchise businesses receive. On the other hand, that means the organization has a weighty opinion on how the franchises are run.

> One example Griswold gave was when the company decided to serve breakfast all day. It was a decision lauded by owners for increasing profitability, but franchisees were required to make significant changes to their kitchens and buy a specific toaster. Had that decision been left to the individual franchisees, they could have simply chosen the toaster they wanted and purchased it.[24]

This might seem like a small detail to be enforced through the SYSTEM, but McDonald's learned long ago specificity brings benefits when knowledge saves time, money, and repair costs down the road—plus the standardization of equipment factors in to maintenance support at a future date. The next 16 franchise examples cover both categories of Yield—the gathering of Knowledge as well as the Comply and Produce required in deploying it well.

1. Slushy Bulk Buy, Anyone? -- Larger franchisors offer bulk buy since there is strength in numbers. Add the knowledge to build proprietary products and this develops another customer hook. Some franchisors have built knowledge in this area to create a significant competitive advantage. Circle K displays this core competency by using their knowledge to leverage the advantage. From the Circle K website:

> Circle K has a strong family of proprietary products that provide our franchisees with high-quality, lower-cost goods. Recognized brands with attractive margins mean more money in your pocket per units sold.
>
> Polar Pop. Get your Polar Pop cup at Circle K and fill it up with one of our incredible fountain beverage options!

24. http://www.wealthmanagement.com/business-planning/mcdonald-s-franchisees-niche-clients-accident-and-all-sudden

> Circle K Premium Coffee & Simply Great Coffee. Our globally recognized coffee programs compete in quality and loyalty with the recognized global chains.
>
> Circle K Favorites. Our private label line is the same excellent quality customers are used to but at a much better price. Favorites stand for quality.
>
> Fresh Foods. We've got your hunger covered.[25]

The franchisor also shares that their power buy system allows a franchisee to gain in many other areas including back office and POS systems, equipment, and fixtures.

2. The parts sum up to more -- Mathematically, 1 + 1 = 2. In franchising, some franchisors share across multiple platforms so that 1 + 1 sums up to more than 2. Belfor, 1-800 Water Damage's parent company, has a massive presence in the restoration world. Belfor has business in the restoration, environmental, and technology spaces to name a few. Belfor utilizes its expertise to help 1-800 Water franchisees in many ways, including sending business across its platforms. When a big project could use the expertise of its sister company, Belfor deals in 1-800 Water Damage, adding revenue and profit to its sister company.

3. Synergy -- Certa Pro is part of FirstService Brands, a group of six franchises including California Closets and Paul Davis Restoration.[26] The collection of six brands shares synergies from their businesses, creating best practices that come from various business sectors.

4. The Best of the Best -- Jim Rohn's quote, "You're the average of the five people you spend the most time with" applies to the knowl-

25. http://www.franchise-circlek.com/why-circle-k
26. http://www.fsvbrands.com/

edge of a franchise network. While the franchisor brings knowledge as the key of the SYSTEM, shared knowledge from top performers offers ways to improve the overall system. From a recent best practice webinar with FranConnect, Dwyer Group CEO Mary Thompson shared that the franchise At the Dwyer Group, the top performers are involved in offering feedback and improving the business as codified practices.[27]

5. Two heads are better than one -- Amazingly, Carlson Wagonlit enjoys 100% attendance at meetings and trainings, according to retired executive Pam Gappa. Of course, a chance to share knowledge and learn from the best often attracts the franchise entrepreneurs. To grow knowledge, Carlson Wagonlit actively engages top performing franchisees through an Advisory Board. Those on the board are elected by their peers, are in good standing with the franchisor, are among the top performers, and they rotate the position to keep fresh input. The Advisory Council meets regularly with face-to-face meetings and quarterly calls, while staying in constant contact with leadership plus attending emergency meetings if required.

Carlson Wagonlit accomplishes this level of nearly 100 % attendance at national meetings—without requiring it in the Franchise Agreement—through offering new information and announcing new programs at these meetings and engaging the top performers to create new knowledge for the franchisees.

6. Technology knowledge leads to greener pastures -- If the purpose of a business is in part to acquire customers who want to come back and do business again, then using knowledge to create a technology that increases retention has great value.

---

27. http://go.franconnect.com/5-best-practices-field-operations-thank-you?submissionGuid=72b66099-9355-4934-95d5-6df711bbe5d5

Customer retention is a key to success for any business, including the franchise industry. When a seasonal business boasts 80% customer retention, business owners take note. According to America's Best Franchises website, America's Best Franchises Lawn Doctor has 80% customer retention that it has earned through a focus on technology and superior customer service. The franchisor notes that with high retention, franchisees are able to use their funds to expand their business instead of using the funds to constantly replace customers. And that is some serious green turf![28]

7. Clipping away with technology -- Knowledge that makes the SYSTEM easier makes life better for all franchisees. And when it also improves the customer experience, well then that is a home run! It takes knowledge of the customer experience to create those tools that accomplish both goals: simplification and customer delight.

Great Clips uses technology to keep their model simple. A digital database called Clip Notes allows stylists to review technical information about a customer's previous clips, and check in becomes a breeze with the ability for customers to check in right from their phones. The check-in app has over five million downloads. The simplicity in technology is considered a contributor to 48 consecutive months of growth and helping the franchise grow to 4,000 locations.[29]

8. 600 years and counting -- Experience rises as one key reason that individuals look to a franchise opportunity versus going DIY. In a franchise system, typically the experience equates to efficiency and profitability. At Liberty Tax Service, the executive team boasts over 600 years of experience in its industry. A vast number of years of knowledge offers an operating system packed with great insight.

---

28. http://www.americasbestfranchises.com/home-services/lawn-doctor

29. https://www.greatclips.com/-/media/great-clips/dotcom/files/news-room/precision-cut_shopping-centers-today_120116.pdf

Six hundred years is about 2.5 times the age of our country—that's some serious experience![30]

9. Expert access -- Some franchises are so specialized that when a franchisor appeals to a prospect, the prospect has great concerns due to the lack of industry experience and inability to gain that expertise even with training. While many franchisors seek general experience over industry specific experience, the prospect's concerns over the specialized industry present a real roadblock on closing the deal. With that knowledge, Monster Tree decided to eliminate the concern and keep the franchisee focused on running the business.[31]

Typically, the franchisee, who operates as the CEO, performs much better working across the entire business ensuring that all tasks from customer acquisition to customer service to customer retention are executed than the subject expert who focuses on serving just one customer at a time. The former has purchased a business, the later only purchased a job. To help franchisees without industry experience hire qualified staff, Monster Tree has an arborist interview as well as background check potential hires for local franchisees. What a confidence builder!

10. Knowing what you need -- Often with DIY, it takes a while to figure out what moves the needle and what lacks return on investment. With a franchise, Key Performance Indicators show where to focus, but in some cases, it still can be difficult to follow or track the key piece. Some franchisors understand that and keep a simple approach to help the franchisee know where to focus.

Order Up has key performance areas like new users per week and order conversion reports that help the franchisee diagnose their business. Mark Johnson, CEO and Founder of Franchise This, shares that success occurs when these reports are clear and monitored.

30. https://www.libertytaxfranchise.com/franchise-support/

31. https://www.monsterfranchising.com/faqs

As the saying goes, garbage in, garbage out. And if the report is too difficult to read or find, then it may as well as not exist.

Comply and Produce comes after the knowledge is shared. It is one thing to know what to do, yet another to do it and produce. Some franchisors have tools and tips that help keep franchisees on task of living their dreams. "What you think about, you bring about," reminds Rhonda Byrne. Make it easy to focus on what moves the needle!

Inspect Often. Fastidious monitoring allows franchisees to course correct when a deviation is first occurring and is still small rather than discovering and having to recover from a neglected and major deviation. From an online article in *Entrepreneur* written by Jason Daly:

> Dean Clarino, Teriyaki Madness Franchisee, keeps close tabs on labor and food costs on a daily basis, something many other restaurant franchisees look at only occasionally. "Our [point-of-sale] system gives percentages, and every night I look at lunch, dinner, and our labor costs," he says. "Those numbers help you understand the neighborhood, like what happens when the sun is out and weather patterns. I know exactly how much we sell on Tuesdays—it's scary how consistent it is. You know when to advertise, when to have two cashiers scheduled. It makes the restaurant run better and makes the customers happy."[32]

11. Did it happen? -- Multi-unit owners especially find knowing what happened at the unit level a challenge. One employee may think that something was done by another employee, but perhaps

32. https://www.entrepreneur.com/article/228698

it was not. And if a key performance action missed the mark, then revenue may miss the mark.

Keith Gerson, President of FranConnect, shares that Marco Pizza has had exponential growth through mastery of accountability. If it is not documented, then it did not happen. To ensure proper documentation, or really to ensure execution, the franchisor created a twenty-year agreement with a consulting company to make sure that both corporate-run stores and franchisee-run locations execute key performance drivers.

12. Make a splash! -- Splash and Dash realized that technology can improve system compliance and therefore produce better results. From the franchise website we read:

> The company created and perfected back-office software that makes the logistics of running a business an efficient and expedited process for all shop owners. [Databases for] point of sales, appointment booking, inventory... and much more are all easily accessible.[33]

Not only are the fundamental back-office actions included, but local marketing campaigns and employee systematization are built in to their SYSTEM automation. The unique terminal software offers everything shop owners need to run their business.[34]

13. Follow the SYSTEM -- The next two examples feature franchisors who created unique hooks that appeal to the target customer and encourage repeat business. The hooks become so synonymous with the business that it would cause customer disappointment to abandon and not comply. Executed well, these hooks feed customer flow nicely.

33. https://splashanddashfranchise.com/splash-dash-best-franchise-opportunity/

34. https://splashanddashfranchise.com/four-valentines-day-marketing-ideas-pet-care-franchise/

Five Guys has a famous hook that has to be executed to be a Five Guys[35]. It includes a generous offering of fresh roasted peanuts and extra fries. Customers talk about the fresh peanuts and the bonus fries like they are legends, so compliance with delivering these offerings is a customer satisfaction requirement.

Similarly, guests can smell the cookies a mile away from DoubleTree. Customer David Deal shares:

> My family and I were in southern Illinois last weekend to explore the Cahokia Mounds State Historic Site. After driving for more than four hours from the Chicago area, we arrived at the Doubletree Hotel in Collinsville (just northeast of St. Louis) on an unseasonably warm October afternoon. The hotel lobby looked clean and was attractively appointed, but I expect cleanliness from a Doubletree. When I checked in at the front desk, a smiling clerk named Ricardo asked me how many people were in my party.
>
> "Three," I replied. "Just me, my wife, and my daughter."
>
> Ricardo then presented me with three warm chocolate chip walnut cookies, tucked into tiny paper bags.[36]

Thank you for the lagniappe moment, Ricardo.

The key with both of these is to offer a hook that the franchisor knows will attract the customer and lead to repeat business, plus have talk value. Making sure that the hook is easily replicated and tracked helps the franchisee achieve the desired results.

---

35. https://en.wikipedia.org/wiki/Five_Guys
36. https://superhypeblog.com/entertainment/whats-your-lagniappe

14. Proprietary system to mint customers -- If the system can mint customers, then why not follow it? That is exactly what Two Maids & A Mop created for their franchisees.

What if your pay was determined by your direct customer? Two Maids & A Mop set a mission to clean up common challenges in their industry—employee and customer retention.[37]

The Franchisor created a Pay for Performance Plan that it credits for increasing the pride a cleaning team takes in caring for a home. The customer rates their level of satisfaction with each service on a scale of 1-10. The rating given determines the compensation the cleaning team receives for cleaning the home. The Pay for Performance Plan has been so successful that it has been used for over 10 years. The franchisor notes that the plan creates an ownership mentality in employees, reduces employee turnover, and has increased customer satisfaction.

It is one thing to find customers, something better to have customer retention, but it is an incredible feat to mint customers as true brand ambassadors! Two Maids & A Mop created a trademarked process called The Complete Experience to do just that—turn customers into coveted brand ambassadors.

The process relies on six steps summarized here:

1. Qualify the Prospect with a proprietary lead generation method
2. Attract the Prospect using the core value of customer feedback
3. Convert the Prospect into a Customer with a systemized sales process

37. http://twomaidsfranchise.com/about-two-maids/our-competitive-advantage/

4. Provide Great Customer Service with employees motivated through a pay for performance plan

5. Convert the Customer into a Brand Ambassador through ensuring satisfaction and making public conversations easy for the customer

6. Receive referrals as one customer creates another customer in the public discussion[38]

By complying with this implemented knowledge, franchisees produce results!

15. KPIs on display -- Weed Man, a high-quality lawn care service, publicly displays their use of Key Performance Indicators to help franchisees comply with the system and produce results. From their website:

> In everything we do, there are systems that have been conceived, tested, refined and ultimately proven to increase efficiency and profitability. By taking the time to create standardized procedures, we ensure the ability to duplicate our successes throughout the Weed Man network.
>
> Our systems are based upon measurable results that can be compared across the network to establish benchmarks for success. Proprietary software and algorithms have been created to ensure ease of operation and uniformity in the measurement of our franchisees' results.[39]

38. http://twomaidsfranchise.com/about-two-maids/the-complete-experience/
39. http://weedmanfranchise.com/About/Our-System

16. Stick to your guns -- Pick what matters, publicly promise it, and then deliver. When a franchisor uses knowledge to create difference and then drives it home by a defined measure, it becomes easier to comply and produce.

From sandwich business Capriotti's website you can read their take on sandwich preparation.

> "We are obsessed with food and exceeding expectations." They were ranked the number one Quick Serve Restaurant for Highest Quality and Taste by Sandelman & Associates in a 2014 study. Why? Capriotti's requires restaurants to "prepare our food the hard way":
>
> Slow-Roasted Homemade Turkey
>
> Meatballs Made from Scratch
>
> Homemade Tuna Made Fresh Daily
>
> Premium Grilled Steak & Chicken
>
> Slow-Cooked Hand-Pulled Roast Beef
>
> Fresh Coleslaw Made Daily[40]

The descriptions make your mouth water!

CHAPTER RECAP: YIELD

Franchisees often comment that they join a franchise for the system which includes the knowledge and implementation of that knowledge. Taking best practices to harvest and implement knowledge

40. http://anyflip.com/nisv/vszc/

provides franchisees and franchisors alike the opportunity to produce better results.

CHAPTER 7

START-UP

"The secret to getting ahead is getting started."

— Mark Twain

Starting off on the right foot is a concept from ancient Greece where the left was associated with bad things. Romans adopted the phrase as well, leading to soldiers starting off on the right foot. Steeped in tradition, the phrase stuck and denotes starting off well[41]. Certainly, starting on the "right foot" helps a franchisee immensely.

The following 11 examples show various ways that franchisors help their franchisees start off on the right foot.

1. With a Little Help from my Franchisor -- What happens when the prospect has everything except all of the cash needed to succeed? Some franchisors have created a revenue share model where the franchisor funds large components of the startup package. In this example, 1-800 Water Damage buys equipment plus covers the cost for many other items and benefits. After the initial franchise fee, 1-800 Water Damage tells franchisees to put the checkbook away! The franchisor lowers the ownership risk by buying the trucks and equipment, renting the office, paying the employees, and handling almost all of the back office paperwork. The franchisor also offers a salary, benefits, and 401K plan to owners. From their website:

> After your initial investment you'll continue to receive an income, along with our support, guidance, and training. We even guarantee a first-year minimum income of $30,000 plus a 401(K) and full medical benefits.
>
> Your one-time investment includes:
>
> Franchise fee
>
> 401(K) and full medical benefits

41. http://grammarist.com/idiom/on-the-wrong-foot-on-the-right-foot/

All vehicles, office space, equipment, and insurance needs

Extensive field and classroom training at our state of the art center

Back office support, including payroll, taxes, accounting, and more

Ongoing marketing support and sales assistance[42]

A revenue share situation makes the Franchisee work and the franchisor investment well worthwhile.

2. Start up homework -- Initial training may feel overwhelming. With a fast pace and massive content to learn, absorbing critical pieces challenges the most astute. Some franchisors look for ways to break up the training and start learning prior to ever entering the classroom. According to former franchisee Tim Johnson, CertaPro pre-trains new franchisees.

Prior to attending training, new franchisees complete homework that accelerates their learning during the initial training class. The pre-training includes six webinars that lead to twelve days of class time and six days of field training. CertaPro uses a two-year on boarding process that includes follow up training at various points in the learning curve to maximize the business[43].

Furthermore, classes have a small teacher to student ratio. This continues for the first two years as the franchisee is still considered in training for that period. In addition to a great teacher to student ratio, the franchisor also leverages top performing franchisees as mentors to new franchisees.

42. http://www.belforfranchisegroup.com/1-800-water-damage/investing-in-1-800-water-damage/

43. https://www.franchisedirect.com/directory/certapropainters/ufoc/60/

3. Start up commitment from the top -- Both the franchisee and franchisor make a significant investment with start up.
Imagine a franchisor setting the foundation well by sending their top brass to the franchise location for start up. That act speaks volumes about the franchisor's commitment and willingness to start on the right foot. From Business Franchise Australia online:

> Russell Hampton joined Hire A Hubby after a 24-year career in management at Woolworths. The decision to walk away from a well-paid corporate job was made easier with an income guarantee from Hire A Hubby backing his success as a franchisee. And that success has indeed followed with Russell rapidly growing his Bayview business into the best performing Hire A Hubby franchise nationally.
>
> "When I joined the franchise, Brendan Green, who is the CEO of Hire A Hubby, actually flew up from Sydney to Brisbane, so I had the opportunity to meet him from day one. We worked on a plan from there," says Hampton.[44]

4. Investing in the future -- Start up represents a significant investment. Some franchisees do not understand the magnitude of how it impacts the bottom line of their business. Not every franchisee comes as a seasoned investor. To aid in long-term success and to help with cash flow planning, some franchisors start franchisees with financial experts. From *Entrepreneur* Online: "With Retro Fitness, new Franchisees are assigned a dedicated financial broker to assist prospective franchisees through the execution of strategic funding solutions to support Retro Fitness club development."[45]

44. https://www.businessfranchiseaustralia.com.au/latest-news/qldnt-excellence-franchising-awards-showcase-franchising%E2%80%99s-high-achievers
45. https://www.entrepreneur.com/business-opportunities/164564

5. Teach me to fish -- Similarly, other franchisors teach a franchisee how to understand their finances so that they no longer need a financial translator. Just because the newly minted franchisee has the talent and training to be a franchisee, does not necessarily mean that the newly minted business owner understands how to keep and read financial statements from their own business. Winmark (Play It Again Sports, Style Encore, Plato's Closet, Once Upon a Child, and Music Go Round) franchisees go through a third party training to ensure their understanding of profitability. From the Franchise Direct website:

> **Training and Assistance:** The franchisor conducts its two-part training program at Winmark's training center in Minneapolis. The first session of the training program, New Franchisee Orientation Training (NFOT), covers several aspects of management and operation of a privately-owned retail business, including real estate matters, business plan development, buying used products, Winmark's preferred vendor program, and other topics the franchisor may select. The first part will take place over a period of 5 days. At NFOT, franchisees will be required to participate in an online financial management course conducted by Winmark's third party vendor. This course will educate franchisees on how to understand their financial statements and utilize the information to build their business. The second part of the Plato's Closet training program, Concept Training, is attended after financing and lease are complete. It is conducted over a period of at least 5 days and will include instruction on sales and marketing, merchandising, computer operation, store management, personnel issues and other topics the franchisor selects. The franchisor will not allow

> franchisees to open their Store unless they successfully complete both sessions of the training program.[46]

6. Apprenticeship -- Some franchisors offer an apprenticeship program to aid in the learning process. Jimmy John's incorporates this tactic in their training of new franchisees. From their website:

> All new franchisees participate in a seven-week training program. This program consists of three weeks of Certified Manager Training and four weeks of real-life management experience by way of our Apprenticeship Program in an existing location. Once completed, franchisees receive continuing support, including on-site reviews.[47]

7. Business ownership with a guaranteed salary -- Giving up "steady" income or a regular paycheck challenges many new franchisees. Money Mailer offers a monthly performance check to help franchisees bridge from employment. From their website:

> Giving up a full-time salary prevents some from capturing the business ownership dream. With Money Mailer, a lack of salary is no longer a barrier. Money Mailer provides a monthly performance-based check of $2,000 with the first opening of a virgin unmailed territory. And there is more, Money Mailer covers operating expenses for the first six months plus additional incentives and working capital subsidies for the first two years.[48]

8. Different strokes for different folks -- To grow at a faster pace, some systems have found a SYSTEM for different space re-

---

46. https://www.franchisedirect.com/retailfranchises/platos-closet-franchise-13457/ufoc/
47. https://www.jimmyjohns.com/franchising/common-questions/
48. https://moneymailerfrancise.com/creating-your-success/

quirements or different sizes and configurations of units. This allows more franchisees to join. To expand their footprint and to meet the various needs of current and future franchisees, sweetFrog Frozen Yogurt created different models or footprints.[49] The location models include brick and mortar, non-traditional, and mobile locations. This includes a series of mobile truck and trailer units as well as a military base unit. sweetFrog creates the various models and attributes it to their strong growth. In 2017, they added 44 units which represented a 64% year-over-year increase in franchise development sales.

9. Hot dog to space plans -- Nathan's Famous expands its ability to start up more frequently by offering a wide range of restaurant designs. In some cases, this also allows prospects to start a Nathan's who could not otherwise afford the more expensive layout plan. From their website:

> Franchising is a business concept that allows qualified investors to become part of an established, existing "system." A good way to look at franchising is, you're in business for yourself but not by yourself. Strategically, this provides many benefits under a brand name that has consumer awareness and equity. Nathan's has taken this basic premise and redefined it to exceed the most stringent business criteria of today's investor.[50]

Nathan's offers a wide range of restaurant designs and customized equipment, thereby offering business opportunities to qualified candidates regardless of space constraints or investment limitations.

10. In free -- Dutch Bros. has an adherence to their culture and is willing to put its money where its mouth is. To protect culture, Dutch Bros. adds new franchisees from employees at other loca-

49. http://www.digitaljournal.com/pr/3651111
50. http://franchise.nathansfamous.com/

tions. To that end, Dutch Bros. waives the franchise fee for employees to become owners. To smooth out the start up, the franchisor offers a start up package with many benefits ranging from remodeling to four weeks of help. From the Dutch Bros website:

> The company also took over site development for new franchisees, scoping locations, buying or leasing property, and paying for remodeling or construction of the can't-miss-gray-and-blue Dutch Bros. stands, with their peaked roofs, bas-relief windmills and tulips painted around the base of the exterior. Franchisees get a plug-and-play operation, paying rent to headquarters, which handles payroll and accounting. New equipment, which includes $10,000 La Marzocco espresso machines, can total $150,000, and franchisees must pay $30,000 to $60,000 for opening-day expenses. That includes a celebration with wind socks, giant inflated coffee cups, free drinks to all comers, and a team of up to eight trainers, called Dutch Mobsters, who stay on-site for at least four weeks.[51]

11. Encourage a community -- Recruiting the top franchise prospects is a competitive business. Some franchisors reach out through the community to plant not only the franchise seed but to also leave their concept top of mind. 7-Eleven created a program called "W.E. Take the Lead" free franchise contest to encourage entrepreneurship and scout for talent. Prongs to the program include that free franchise contest and an internship program. [52]

"To achieve these goals, 7-Eleven is increasing partnerships with various non-profit organizations that support Hispanic, African American and veteran entrepreneurs. In addition, we have created

51. https://www.forbes.com/sites/susanadams/2016/06/15/the-coffee-cult-how-dutch-bros-is-turning-its-bro-istas-into-wealthy-franchisees/#6d92832a3694
52. http://franchise.7-eleven.com/franchise-blog/closing-the-gap-in-minority-owned-franchises-part-1

an initiative like the W.E. Take the Lead, a Women's Franchise Giveaway to encourage female business leaders to join the 7-Eleven family in their local communities."

CHAPTER RECAP: YIELD

It is easier to train someone correctly from the beginning. Starting with the end in mind, a Covey principle, the successful franchisor does what it needs to do to break down information to make it more easily absorbed and to take away sticking points that may derail a new franchisee.

CHAPTER 8

TRAINING

"Tell me and I forget,
teach me and I may remember,
involve me and I learn."

– Benjamin Franklin

After setting franchisees up for success with great start up tools and training, continued learning and training will fuel continued success. Those familiar with Stephen Covey's *The 7 Habits of Highly Effective People* recall that Principle 7 is Sharpen the Saw. Covey has a quote that applies to training as a tool to sharpen a franchisee's performance, "If I really want to improve my situation, I can work on the one thing over which I have control—myself." Franchisors with excellent training provide a platform for the franchisees to excel as well as to continue to grow.

Franchise systems operate like a human in that the world around the business changes. Competition rises and folds. Technology changes the way we interact, buy, and even what we need. The franchise learns and grows by adapting to its environment, perhaps shaping the change from the franchise community experiences. In that sense, the franchise system is like an adaptive organism that assimilates experiences from various franchise units and uses the learning to make the SYSTEM stronger. Training remains the tool to deploy the knowledge so that the many franchisees benefit as well as the franchisor. The following 10 examples showcase various approaches to training excellence that may benefit your organization.

1. Success breeds success -- Franchise icon McDonald's has a clear layout for their ongoing training and a quote that shows their passion for their SYSTEM. From their website:

> Our franchising system is built on the premise that McDonald's can be successful only if our Owner/Operators are successful. We believe in a partnering relationship with our Owner/Operators, Suppliers and Employees. Through our world-class training program, you may become a restaurant franchise operational expert focused on providing an outstanding experience for our customers every day.

Training Program Highlights

- 12-18 months training in a restaurant
- Self-directed, part-time training for 20 hours per week
- Seminars, conferences and one-on-one training sessions
- Success based on competency
- Operator training classes conducted by local training professionals[53]

2. Meet me where I am -- The maturity, or the time a franchisee spends in a system, changes the need for training. Some franchisors differentiate training tracks more than just new vs. experience. Ace Hardware shares that it has multiple ways to train franchisees across experience levels as well as franchisee employees. From the Franchise Direct website:

> Ace's New Owners Institute is a required training program offered at the franchisor's headquarters in Oak Brook, Illinois. New Investor Retail Training includes: New Owners Institute (for 2 people), Retail Business Coach, New Associate Training, Inventory Management, Helpful 101 Certification, The Supply Place and Loss Prevention Audit, and Lean Operations.
>
> The franchisor also has voluntary training programs. One of the franchisor's major voluntary training programs is known as Essential Management Skills, and enrollment is open to both new and established mem-

53. https://www.mcdonalds.com/us/en-us/about-us/franchising/training-services.html

> bers. This instructor-led course is intended for store managers and consists of approximately two consecutive days of training on various leadership topics including time management, delegation skills and more.
>
> The franchisor's most popular voluntary training session is the Pinnacle Performance Retailing (PPR) Workshop. It is designed for owners, managers and assistant managers who want to strategically align their leadership focus with the performance drivers in 20/20 Vision. This 3.5-day program is structured around the 5 P's of Retail.
>
> The newest voluntary training session is CHAMP (Certified Helpful Ace Management Program). This 6 to 9 month program is intended for managers, potential managers and owners and results in an Ace Hardware Management Certification.
>
> The franchisor periodically schedules training sessions and seminars for individual retailers and retailer groups. The franchisor also provides training sessions and workshops on topics of interest to store owners and managers twice a year at its spring and autumn conventions[54].

3. I'm here! -- Circle K also offers training for the franchisee at different levels of experience and for the franchisee's employees as well. From their website:

> Our training programs utilize proven best-practices to empower you with the knowledge required to operate your stores successfully.

54. https://www.franchisedirect.com/retailfranchises/ace-hardware-corporation-06448/ufoc/

SMART Academy – A comprehensive program which combines classroom learning and in-store experience.

NETP (New Employee Training Program) – An eight-module, downloadable program provided to assist you in training your new employees.

Smart STEP – A four-step, advanced program provided to assist you in developing your store staff's management potential.

Continued Learning – Our Training Team, along with your Franchise Business Consultant, will continue to work with you to keep you up to date on the latest operational and marketing best-practices.[55]

4. Two paths -- Mary Thompson, CEO of Dwyer Group runs a franchise operation that attracts franchisees from two different paths. One comes from business professionals and the other comes from those currently working in the trade skill of the franchise. From a webinar with FranConnect[56] Mary shares, "At the Dwyer Group, their collection of franchises attracts franchisees from different perspectives. Some are business people while others are tradesmen. Dwyer understands that different backgrounds require different training areas to ensure success."

5. Edible training - To offer a great customer experience, training franchisees and employees holds particular importance. And in a world where competitors constantly raise the bar, ongoing training is paramount to success. So, at Edible Arrangements, training terminals have been added to all locations. Edible Arrangements calls them Inspire Terminals, as they wish to inspire all employees. The

55. http://www.franchise-circlek.com/why-circle-k

56. http://go.franconnect.com/5-best-practices-field-operations-thank-you?submissionGuid=72b66099-9355-4934-95d5-6df711bbe5d5

terminals have detailed step by step instructions to make standout arrangements. The terminals offer a supplement to annual trainings at Edible Arrangements corporate location.[57]

6. See You at Headquaters - Franchisees often appreciate corporate employees that walk a day, or weeks, in their shoes. At Edible Arrangements, the franchisor regularly invites franchisees to the corporate store, even paying for the hotel costs. This helps when new features are rolled out across the franchise system. The process also helps to get franchisee input and buy-in so new products are not seen as forced upon them.[58]

7. It takes a team -- Many franchisors require the franchisee to successfully complete training before granting franchise rights. To insure that the franchisee is off to a good start, Wendy's takes it a step further and makes sure that the franchisee's team, not just the manager but the employees also, successfully pass training to open. From the Franchise Direct site:

> Training Overview: Before the opening of the Restaurant, franchisees (or, if the franchisee is a corporation, partnership, or other business entity, the Operator for the Restaurant as previously approved by the franchisor) and their initial management employees and Restaurant crew must attend and complete, to the franchisor's satisfaction, an initial training program. At the franchisor's option, any management persons later employed by the franchisee must also attend and complete the training program, to the franchisor's satisfaction. Franchisees and their management employees involved in the operation of the Restaurant must also attend additional courses, seminars, and other training programs as the franchisor may reasonably require. A

57. https://www.entrepreneur.com/article/283277

58. https://www.entrepreneur.com/article/283277

typical initial training program will be approximately 20-24 weeks in duration and will include online, classroom, virtual instructor led and on-the-job training. Training is conducted at various certified training Restaurants throughout the United States. The franchisor also offers and may require additional training programs.[59]

8. Constant growth -- Club Pilates offers conventions and training classes plus helps with recruitment and human resources, two issues that generally garner the most concern from potential and new franchisees. From their website:

TRAINING & SUPPORT

- Annual convention
- Teacher Training program
- Strong brand management
- Training manuals & videos
- Recruitment support
- Hiring and HR assistance
- Manager & sales rep training
- Real estate assistance[60]

9. Am I licensed? -- Some franchises require more than SYSTEM training; they require a license or special credential. This requirement could be a sticking point, but for some franchises it becomes a

59. https://www.franchisedirect.com/foodfranchises/wendys-franchise-08373/ufoc
60. http://www.clubpilatesfranchise.com/why-club-pilates/

sales point as they offer the opportunity to obtain a credential that may become a barrier to entry for DIY. This is the case with Dream Vacations. And for continuous learning, the franchise boasts 500 different online training modules. From their website:

> **Travel Agent Training and Support**
>
> At Dream Vacations Franchise, we're proud to offer our franchisees award-winning travel agent training and ongoing support that builds a foundation for success. After attending a six-day initial training at our world headquarters in the cruise capital of the world, you'll have access to more than 500 online training modules that include product courses covering itineraries, cruise lines, resort and tour vendors, and technology tips as well as sales soft skills training and introductory-level refresher classes. We also hold various regional training and immersive summits throughout the year to help franchise owners boost sales, and we have developed a franchisee Business Center that you can use to connect with your community of home-based travel agency business owners.
>
> **How to Become a Travel Agent**
>
> If you're wondering how to be a travel agent, consider starting your career with Dream Vacations Franchise. Though a high school diploma or GED is needed in order to operate successfully in the business world, you don't have to worry about obtaining training or credentials prior to joining the Dream Vacations Franchise family. Once you become a franchise owner, you'll attend a training seminar that prepares you with the tools and knowledge you need to launch a successful career as a travel agent. And with access to

resources that would be hard to secure independently, the Dream Vacation Franchise is able to provide you with around-the-clock support that helps you navigate the travel agency industry.[61]

10. Straight from the Horse's Mouth-- During a recent webinar with FranConnect,[62] Justin Waltz, Founder of Peer Performance Groups and author of *Disrupt from Within* shared a strategy to accelerate performance – Peer Performance Groups. While this could also be a form of support, Peer Performance Groups serve as motivation and provide a chance for franchisees to share knowledge among themselves. Therefore, it can also become a type of peer training. As Justin shared, franchisees would rather hear it from each other than hear it from their Franchise Business Coach. During the same webinar, Jeff Bevis, Co-Founder and CEO of First-Light HomeCare Franchising LLC, shared that his organization posts Key Performance Indicator information monthly right on the home page of the owners' franchise website. This fosters not only competition but also the chance to connect with others who excel in one area where you wish to improve.

CHAPTER RECAP: TRAINING

Training takes the franchise SYSTEM knowledge and packages it in a way that takes the franchisor and franchisee to a new level. Whether it is a system with numerous offerings, a specialty training, building training that meets a franchisee where they are, or pairing top performers with others, franchisors seek unique ways to deliver training in a more meaningful way.

61. https://www.dreamvacationsfranchise.com/travel-agent-training/

62. http://go.franconnect.com/best-practices-maximizing-franchisee-unit-profitability

CHAPTER 9

ENGAGEMENT AND CULTURE

"Culture is simply a shared way of doing something with a passion."

– Brian Chesky, Co-Founder, CEO, Airbnb

Engagement creates a receptive franchise community that actively follows the SYSTEM as well as paves a way to expansion in terms of units and unit performance. Proper execution delivers higher value to the customer and stickier retention that delivers more profits for both the franchisee and franchisor.

Culture, at the core, differentiates you from your competition both to attract a potential franchisee as well as to attract and retain customers. Proper franchisee selection will make engagement and culture preservation easier as fewer forces exist to tear it apart.
While the franchisor creates the Culture, franchisees show their Engagement in the business with the "passion" exhibited when they execute that Culture. Often, as in the Chick-fil-A example, we know that the customer experience is influenced by the culture of a franchise and that customers should 'feel' the culture as part of their experience. Typically, showcasing the culture creates a point of difference for the customer, giving them a reason to choose you over the competition. This section carries a mix of 13 franchisor and franchisee level examples that show dedication to Culture and how franchisees go above and beyond to demonstrate it with high levels of Engagement.

1. Put your headquarters where your brand lives -- An *Entrepreneur* online article shared how Maui Wowi went so far as to move their headquarters to better align their corporate culture with delivering their brand experience. Contributor Jason Daly wrote:

> Last winter, Maui Wowi Hawaiian Coffees & Smoothies moved its headquarters from the Denver Tech Center.... Instead of setting up drab cubicles, CEO Mike Weinberger insisted the [new] office be decked out with surfboards and faux palm trees. The 14 corporate employees and 200 franchisees of the system, who run 450 units, are encouraged to wear Hawaiian

> shirts and flip-flops whenever sensible. "Culture, from our employee and franchisee standpoint, is one of the most important things we do," Weinberger says. "We want to create a sense of belonging and purpose, especially when we're not sitting next to our franchisees every day. That's hard to get across. We want to send out a tribe mentality."[63]

2. Bros. mafia -- Some franchisors have culture that runs so deep that it has been referred to as mafia like. In a Forbes article by Susan Adams, members of the Dutch Bros. (pronounced Brose) franchise share thoughts on their culture and how they engage to live it every day. From the article:

> Dutch Bros., based in Grants Pass, Oregon, hires and promotes only outgoing optimists committed to customer service. No bad tempers allowed. 'It's our Dutch Bros. way of life,' Kristen Von Tersch, a franchisee, says, 'practicing love and humility.'
>
> 'Other coffee establishments are all about the coffee or about the ambience of sitting in the shop,' says Joshua Margolis, a professor of organizational behavior at Harvard Business School who wrote a case study on the company in 2014. 'Dutch Bros.' culture revolves around the connections they make with their people.'
>
> 'We simply don't tolerate toxic or cancerous behavior to the culture,' says Travis Boersma, Dutch Bros.' CEO and cofounder.[64]

63. https://www.entrepreneur.com/article/253840
64. https://www.forbes.com/sites/susanadams/2016/06/15/the-coffee-cult-how-dutch-bros-is-turning-its-bro-istas-into-wealthy-franchisees/

3. A group for everyone -- Involving franchisees and obtaining their input engages the franchise system and weaves in franchisees as part of the culture's fabric. McDonald's, one of the world's best-known franchisors, utilizes many committees to make sure that top performers have input from around the company. From their website, the list includes:

> McDonald's National Leadership Council, National Black McDonald's Operator Association, McDonald's Hispanic Operator Association, Women's Operator Network, McDonald's Owner Operator Pride Network and Asian McDonald's Operator Association provide a national forum for the exchange of ideas between the Company and its Owner / Operators. Divisional and Regional Leadership Councils, local advertising co-ops, and regional business meetings also provide valuable interaction at the local level. As a McDonald's Owner / Operator, you will experience a unique relationship with the Company—one that is unparalleled in the quick service restaurant industry. McDonald's leadership position continues to be built on the respect the Company shows its Owner / Operators.[65]

4. Protecting the Culture -- Equally important, the Franchisor must protect culture. And if provisions are not in place, then course correction can cause uncomfortable situations. The Dwyer Group has several concepts including: AireServ, Five Star Painting, Glass Doctor, The Grounds Guys, Mr. Appliance, Mr. Electric, Mr. Handyman, Mr. Rooter, Molly Maid, Portland Glass, Protect Painters, Rainbow International Restoration, Locatec, Window Genie, Bright & Beautiful, Countrywide Grounds Maintenance, Drain Doctor, and Real Property Management. During a webinar hosted by FranConnect at, Mary Thompson, the CEO of the Dwyer

---

65. https://www.mcdonalds.com/us/en-us/about-us/franchising/support-system.html

Group, shared that sticking to the core values is essential. If an employee or franchisee catches another, even a member of the C-suite, doing something that does not live up the values, then they are to immediately tell someone.[66]

5. Lifestyle brand's culture -- Culture may also come in the form of how the franchise operates as lifestyle is one element of culture. With the fitness franchise ILoveKickBoxing.com, the franchisor offers a SYSTEM that supports a certain lifestyle. The lifestyle is part of the culture as well as part of the selection process. Often would-be-franchisees look to ownership, specifically franchise ownership, to provide additional time with their family. With a range of results, some find new lifestyles that leave the neighbors envious for their work week. According to ILoveKickBoxing.com franchisee Peter Peck, he has turned over about 85% of his workload to employees. Walter Rowe has a similar tale, offering that he works five-hours per week on the business, leaving plenty of time for family. Now that is an unbalanced work week most would envy.[67]

6. Costa Vida mission focused -- Seeding the company's mission at a corporate office challenges many businesses. With a franchise, seeding it to the franchisee as well as the franchise employees proves demanding work. So, imagine that you are an hourly employee working in a franchised location, and the CEO of the franchise asks you about the company mission. While many would start to sweat at this point, franchise employees of Costa Vida remain cool. In an *Entrepreneur* online article, contributor Jason Daly shared this about Costa Vida, a Salt Lake City restaurant franchise with a Fresh Mexican theme:

---

66. http://go.franconnect.com/5-best-practices-field-operations-thank-you?submissionGuid=72b66099-9355-4934-95d5-6df711bbe5d5
67. www.myilovekickboxing.com/success_stories.php

> Dave Rutter, president, believes culture is what truly animates his business.
>
> Each year, general managers who reach their goals are invited on a company vacation. In 2015, more than 80 managers, franchisees, and other staff members went to Lake Powell on the Arizona-Utah border, where they had a chance to get to know and understand each other outside the office.
>
> 'It definitely changes relationships,' Rutter explains. 'Sometimes you have to have hard conversations when numbers aren't being hit or guests aren't being served correctly. It's easier to have those conversations after you've developed friendships and spent a morning with someone in a fishing boat or on the beach.'[68]

7. **You can change the course of your life with your words** -- At Carlson Wagonlit, franchisees are not called such, but rather are referred to as associates. Pam Gappa, a retired Carlson Wagonlit executive, shares that it created a positive mental picture for corporate employees as well as the associates.

Perhaps it may seem just semantics, but upon further inspection, maybe there is something to word choice. Franchisee is defined by businessdictionary.com as "One who purchases a franchise. The franchisee runs that location of the purchased business. He or she is responsible for certain decisions, but many other decisions are already determined by the franchisor... ."[69] In contrast, Dictionary.com defines associate as "connect (someone or something) with something else in one's mind; a partner or colleague in business or at work; joined or connected with an organization or business."

---

68. https://www.entrepreneur.com/article/253840

69. http://businessdictionary.com/definition/franchisee.html

We have learned from best practices that engagement as well as franchisee feedback fuels growth, so perhaps the difference in definition amounts to more than semantics. The mind shift from franchisee to associate may create a deeper working relationship that shares success accountability between the franchisor and franchisee.

8. A colorful example -- Some franchisees create customer experiences so colorful that they paint a perfect picture of the franchisor's culture. This perfect picture was shared by Jed Langdon from a comment on the post "What's Your Purple Goldfish?"

> My girlfriend's father is a HUGE Pizza Express fan, and I can now understand why. I'm not sure if you have Pizza Express in the US, but it is a large Pizza restaurant franchise with over 300 restaurants in the UK (it is called Pizza Marzano in some other countries). He visits his local Pizza Express on average about once a fortnight and is on first name terms with a lot of the staff there. When he walks in the chef usually begins to make his favorite dish, but what is even more impressive is that this is a starter that is no longer on the menu. This is a relationship that has been built up over time through him visiting the restaurant and not because he knows any of the staff, which is often the reason for a customer getting this treatment.
>
> Anyway, a couple of weeks ago, my girlfriend's father was admitted to hospital (fortunately, he is going to be ok) and on hearing about him being in hospital the manager of his local Pizza Express took it upon herself to surprise him with his favorite pizza! She contacted the Pizza Express which was closest to the hospital and asked them to make and deliver the pizza to the hospital, free of charge. This is one of the kindest and most generous acts I have seen from a business, and nobody

> had expected this sort of thought and effort. Talk about making a customer feel valued, special, and delivering service way above and beyond expectations![70]

9. A Whataburger Baby Shower -- Whataburger in Birmingham, Alabama, also painted a perfect picture of franchise culture. Hailey Daughtery was seven-months pregnant and not living in a state with her food craving—Whataburger. Daughtery went to social media with her craving and a received a big surprise. Whataburger sent an SUV to her home in Nashville and drove her and her girlfriends to the closest Whataburger almost four-hours away. They not only satisfied her cravings but also threw a baby shower for Daughtery! Craving solved and WhataSurprise![71]

10. Illuminating culture -- There is never a better test of a culture than a crisis. When a hurricane hit LaPorte, Texas, many were left without the basic necessities for daily life. A local Liberty Tax Service franchisee opened her heart and her office offering residents a place to charge their phones or tablets, chilled drinks, and a place for kids to be entertained by watching a movie. This provided local families a moment of reprieve from the flood and destruction.[72]

11. Community impact -- While some crises affect a community, others deeply impact one member of the team. And how fellow franchisees respond speaks volumes for the franchise's culture. As reported in the *Over the Mountain Journal* of Vestavia Hills, Alabama:

> When Marty Abercrombie, a Wing Zone Franchisee, faced the unthinkable when his son, Ben, was paralyzed in his first football game at Harvard, the Franchisor stepped up with national support. On a day in December, everyone who would donate $1 to a sup-

70. http://theexperiencefactor.com/whats-your-purple-goldfish/795/

71. https://stories.whataburger.com/a-bump-in-the-road/

72. https://www.facebook.com/photo.php?fbid=10213634728840121&set=a.1584344286111.2080108.1160868463&type=3&theater

> porting fund received 5 free wings for their donation. It is wonderful when the franchisors and franchisees come together to support one of their own!
>
> 'Our franchisees come first at Wing Zone, and when we heard about Ben's injury and the impact this was having on Marty and his family, we banded together to come up with a way to help support them while also giving back to our Flavorholics in the middle of the holiday season,' said Matt Friedman, co-founder and CEO of Wing Zone.[73]

12. Windows to the soul -- If eyes are the windows to the soul, then charitable acts serve as windows to a franchisor's culture. With sweetFrog Frozen Yogurt's "Deck the Halls" program, the community benefits and their culture shines. From an online article in *Broadway World*:

> As part of the "Deck the Halls" event, each participating sweetFrog shop will help the choir raise funds while providing each member with a free frozen yogurt. And for parents, grandparents, neighbors, friends, and other choir supporters who come to enjoy the music, sweetFrog will donate a portion (25% recommended) of the sales from all items purchased by those guests while the choir is performing.
>
> "All of us at sweetFrog love this annual event that gets us in the Christmas spirit," said sweetFrog's CEO, Patrick Galleher. "It's a wonderful time of community fellowship as people come together to celebrate Christmas. What better way to do that than enjoying the sounds of the season sung by local choirs? We are

73. http://www.otmj.com/wing-zone-ben-abercrombie/

> proud to showcase great local talent and support local churches and schools, while helping our sweetFrog owners generate some serious winter foot traffic!"[74]

13. The power of one -- Many franchisors who listen to franchisee feedback find gold. In this case, Firehouse Subs listened to franchisee Windy Griffin to form a national charity. Griffin's operation is more about building a community than building a business. With no restaurant experience, she and her husband, Jerry, have grown the number of Firehouse units in their home market of Phoenix from one in 2011 to five locations as of 2018. The duo also launched Firehouse's H2O for Heroes program, which began as a local endeavor and is now a system-wide initiative that provides bottled water to first responders. In Summer 2017, 1,090 restaurants participated collecting more than 35,000 cases of water.[75]

CHAPTER RECAP: ENGAGEMENT AND CULTURE

A defined and well protected culture helps attract the right people and gives them a reason to engage, even in tough situations. Naturally, people are attracted and engaged when the mission ties to their core values. A united culture and engaged franchisee base fuels growth.

---

74. https://www.broadwayworld.com/bwwfood-wine/article/Deck-the-Halls-Christmas-Spectacle-Returns-to-sweetFrog-Frozen-Yogurt-20171213
75. https://www.qsrmagazine.com/franchising/how-franchisees-inspired-firehouse-subs-give-back

CHAPTER 10

MANAGING

"Help others achieve their dreams
and you will achieve yours."

- Les Brown

Managing has two parts. The first part focuses upon Support, the managing the business and operations of the business. The second part deals with Advertising that includes customer acquisition, branding, and managing the brand. With Manage, the franchisor and franchisee have to manage the business (Support) and manage the customer experience from start to finish (Advertising, in short). Combine Support and Advertising and this area focuses upon the acquisition, retention, and delight of customers.

Support stands out as one of the franchisee expectations from day one. And some franchisors have tackled the task of not only providing support but also making the franchisee feel supported in unique ways. Sometimes, the franchisor provides adequate support, but perception is reality. It's important to make the franchisees feel well supported. This section covers the confluence of great support plus leaving the franchisee feeling supported. The next 11 examples create a picture of Support.

1. Putting the Pieces Together -- As many franchises are owned by spouses or business partners, the thought of losing the other partner may evoke fear—fear of picking up the specialized areas that the other covered and simply picking up more workload. In this case, the franchisor, FISH Window Cleaning, jumped right in to help bridge the great loss. From an *Entrepreneur* article by Julie Bennett:

> Susan Smith, a franchisee of FISH, shares her story of the ultimate support. She and her husband, Doug, purchased a franchise and Doug ran the businesses. A fatal heart attack left Susan a widow and primary business owner. FISH Corporate stayed after the funeral to help Smith learn the business, and a district manager traveled several hours to aid as well. Franchising fortunately offers the opportunity for this type of help

> that does not exist with DIY. Smith indicates that she has been able to grow the business since and has been named franchisee of the year by the company.[76]

Top franchisors will step up when the chips are down.

2. Can I get a hand or blouse? -- To offer franchisees continuous support, Scout & Molly's Boutique assigns a skilled buyer assigned to every franchisee. This buyer customizes the clothing selections for the store, so each collection is different than other franchised locations. The buyer takes into account weather, customer preferences, and other data to aid the franchisee in having the right product mix for each individual store and the right inventory levels.

3. Tutoring for the Tutor -- A franchisee is not an expert in every facet of their business. It is not uncommon, for example, for a franchisee to need help with customer acquisition. To gain new customers, Tutor Doctor sends marketing experts to each territory.

> Many businesses and franchises thrive by building bonds with other local businesses. To help their franchisees, Tutor Doctor sends an expert to the local market to build relationships with local schools and organizations to build the franchisee's business.

4. Grow together -- It is a great job to coach but without accountability for forward momentum, coaching is incomplete. What if the coach has more skin in the game? To create a win-win-win (corporate-franchisee-customer), Buzz Brands holds their franchise coaches accountable for franchisee results and goal achievement.[77]

5. Takes one to know one -- Lower ratios of franchisees to coaches plus experienced staff will fuel growth. Mosquito Joe, part

76. https://www.entrepreneur.com/article/217715
77. http://go.franconnect.com/webinar-ceo-secrets-watch-now?submissionGuid=beddcfab-635c-46c9-8c61-33f973d9fa81

of Buzz Brands, assigns a franchise business coach before the first training. Coaches are solid in the business, financial planning, and understand people as well as profit and loss statements. Coaches use weekly calls and contests for customer recruitment as tools to motivate and train new franchisees.[78]

6. Because I Said So -- With any business, giving your word and holding to it goes miles toward customer satisfaction. And a fulfilled written guarantee is like money in the bank. According to franchise consultant Pete Tucker, Shelf Genie uses a pledge card to explain their commitment to potential franchisees. The card says, "Because I Said So." An example is one employee promises to call the franchisee back within 10 minutes, "Because I Said So." The Franchisee keeps the cards with the extraordinary promises.

7. It's my honor -- Some franchisors count working in operations as "just" a promotion. At Carlson Wagonlit, it is an honor to have a position in Operations. Employees work their way up to an operations position where former employee Pam Gappa says that franchisees offered a 95% satisfaction rating with their support levels—a franchise service high!

8. It's Within Your Reach -- Depending up the franchise, you may hear that it is difficult to gain commercial customers or even government accounts, yet the profit from those customers often exceeds smaller private jobs. 1-800 Water Damage's parent company, Belfor, has a massive presence in the restoration world, and Belfor utilizes its expertise to help 1-800 Water franchisees. As one example, Belfor completes Third Party Account (TPA) paperwork, a complex process for those new to restoration, to help new franchisees take advantage of business opportunity. Now that is teamwork![79]

---

78. http://go.franconnect.com/webinar-ceo-secrets-watch-now?submissionGuid=beddcfab-635c-46c9-8c61-33f973d9fa81
79. http://www.belforfranchisegroup.com/1-800-water-damage/why-1-800-water-damage/

9. Experience the Difference -- One SYSTEM key includes experience. A prospective franchisee will consider the model itself and the franchisor team's experience as a significant part of deciding to join a franchise. Depth of relevant experience—both a tried and true SYSTEM and corporate executive experience in the model—can differentiate between franchise offerings. In an interview, Wayback Burgers' Executive Vice President, Bill Chemero, and other Wayback C-level executives discussed the importance of having executives who can leverage their previous franchise experience into success for the company nationwide. From the Wall Street Journal article as featured on Franchising.com:

> In his conversation with Wall Street Journal franchising reporter, Julie Bennett, Wayback Burgers EVP Bill Chemero analyzed Wayback Burgers' progress from when he and President and CEO John Eucalitto purchased the franchise to where it is today.
>
> [Chemero said] "Wayback Burgers is prospering in part because of the leadership's strong franchising experience.
>
> "There are several factors contributing to Wayback Burgers' rapid growth," says Chemero. "John and I have more than 60 combined years of experience in franchising. We understand the importance of our franchisees and how to make our company and brand appealing to potential franchise partners interested in joining the Wayback family.
>
> "Not only that, but we understand how to capitalize on cutting edge food trends that appeal to our guests, helping our franchise partners generate more in-store traffic. We're proud of what we've accomplished, and

> we're excited about what the future has in store for everyone at Wayback!"[80]

10. A fine line -- A franchise offers a delicate balance between a system to follow and business ownership. To tip too much one way is to be an employee again. To tip too much to "own" your ownership dilutes the benefit of following a proven system. With support, there is a balance, a delicate dance between the two... from a Small Biz Trends article by Mark O'Neill:

> As a UPS Store franchise owner, you might wonder how much freedom you have. Brett Robertson insists that it's very much up to each individual store owner to make a success of their franchise business.
>
> You aren't taking orders from the franchise headquarters. "Yes, you have to follow certain rules, such as how a store is laid out and the products and services you sell in it. And you pay a small royalty to the franchisor. But aside from that, it's really all on the individual owner," he added.
>
> When first setting out, the franchisor sends the franchisee designs of how the store should be laid out, and where each thing—such as displays—should go. This is to ensure that a customer can get the same experience regardless of which store they visit. The franchisor also designates tools and software needed to do the job, such as credit card processing software.
>
> Otherwise, the franchisor lets owners like Robertson get on with running the show.[81]

80. https://www.franchising.com/news/20180515_wayback_burgers_featured_in_wall_street_journalrsq.html
81. https://smallbiztrends.com/2014/12/robertson-owning-a-ups-store-franchise.html

11. In the blink of an eye -- When you want enhanced quality relative to the competition, create your own! And some franchisors do just that with proprietary products that support the franchisee through quality, use, installation, and so forth. For example, Amazing Lash offers a Patented Eyelash Application Process. From their website:

> **Patented Eyelash Application Process**
>
> As a pioneer of the industry, Amazing Lash Studio has developed innovative processes and procedures that have improved the market. Amazing Lash Studio has been awarded a patent for its proprietary application process that helps lash stylists decrease the time required for a service and also improve the durability of the lashes. Saving our guests time and increasing how long their lashes last drives customer loyalty and repeat visits.
>
> **Proprietary Contemporary Styles**
>
> In addition to our patented processes, Amazing Lash Studio has also been awarded a patent for its contemporary lash styles. Guests can choose from four unique styles: Natural, Cute, Sexy and Gorgeous. These styles are then customized to fit our guests' eye shape, contour and personal preference. The result is amazing—most guests are so delighted [that] they check out their new look multiple times in mirrors throughout the studio on their way out; and our stylists feel pride in their work, because our lash styles are unique and create a natural look they know their guests will love. Only Amazing Lash Studio has patented styles.[82]

---

82. https://franchising.amazinglashstudio.com/amazing-opportunity/why-amazing-lash

ADVERTISING

The holy grail of most businesses—customer acquisition, delight the customer, and hopefully repeat many times! Sometimes this happens through the power of the brand. Other times it may include a unique hook, a well-articulated point of difference, or an execution twist. Franchisees seek this as part of the SYSTEM, and some franchisors are delivering customer after customer.

Franchisees need ways that they too can express their passion. Through this passion, the franchisee can build lasting relationships with customers who want to exchange financial currency for the emotional currency. In this section, we will share 10 examples of ways to think about the Advertising component. In our Bonus section, we will share many ideas of how to create those valuable emotional bonds with customers that build strong programs to acquire, delight, and retain.

1. The 800-pound gorilla on your side -- McDonald's is the king of franchising, so let's take a look at what McDonald's promises franchisee -- a SYSTEM! These points were taken directly from McDonald's website:

> Being a McDonald's Owner / Operator offers you many advantages—from the training and the support of a solid organization, to the opportunity to own a thriving and successful business. Essentially, here's what you receive ...[with] the benefits of franchising as a McDonald's Owner / Operator:
>
> - Use of the trademarks and operating system of one of the best-known brands in the world.
>
> - The tools to help you in your business: local and national support in the areas of operations, training, advertising, marketing, human resources, real

estate, construction, purchasing, and equipment purchasing and maintenance.

- The opportunity to contribute to the success of McDonald's: Big Mac®, Filet-O-Fish®, and Egg McMuffin® sandwiches have all been developed by Owner / Operators.[83]

2. 80% in the bag! -- Customer acquisition keep many business owners up at night. To reduce these worries, franchisors spend numerous resources building this part of the SYSTEM. Help with customer acquisition is a big reason to go franchise and not to go DIY. Some franchisors take customer acquisition as their task and provide a large chunk of customers to the franchisee. The Cleaning Authority cleans up on that worry for franchisees with a marketing program that drives approximately 80% of local customer acquisition. TCA combines tools like direct mail, digital strategy, and other tools to drive business forward.[84]

3. Make the phone ring -- As business owners know, making the phone ring is not free. So, when the call comes in, the owner wants the sale closed. To aid in call conversion, AdvantaClean Corporate Call Center takes all calls for franchisees. This removes pressure on the franchisee, especially in the start-up phase.

4. Mr. Roboto goes smoothie -- The size and scale of some franchises allow them to develop technology to aid in the customer acquisition, delight, and retention area faster than a DIY option. The bright, colorful robotic vending machines at Alberts Smoothie Stations uses technology to retain customers. From an online article in The Spoon, Co-Founder and CTO Glenn Mathijssen shares:

83. https://www.mcdonalds.com/us/en-us/about-us/franchising/support-system.html

84. http://franchise.thecleaningauthority.com/training-support/marketing-experts/

> Out of the box, the Alberts Smoothie Station has six menus, but you can customize them to your liking if you download their app. For instance, you can specify that you want more mango and less banana, or more vitamin C. Using a QR code in the app, a Smoothie Station can 'recognize you and already know how to prepare your preferred drink.
>
> Additionally, Alberts gives users the options of connecting their calendars to its system, so the Smoothie Stations will know if you just exercised and can ping you with a suggestion for a thirst-quenching blend. Mathijssen said the company is looking at additional ways of connecting Smoothie Stations with devices like your phone or FitBit to automatically know who you are and any activity you might have partaken in, but there are privacy considerations to address...[85]

5. Tech to retain -- Technology plays can catapult a business when a national player applies the scope and skill to leverage technology. From an online magazine article in PMQ Pizza Magazine by Liz Barrett regarding an interview with Firenza Pizza CEO Dave Baer:

> We are very heavy into social media. We have a strong presence on Facebook, Twitter and Instagram, and we're testing Snapchat filters that are giving our business a lot of traction. We can geotarget a specific area and send them an offer using Snapchat filters. We did one at the end of the school day that got more than 800 shares in a matter of hours. Once school let out, the store was bombarded.

85. https://thespoon.tech/alberts-brings-robot-smoothie-stations-to-europe/

> We've also started playing with Waze, the navigation app from Google. We have it set up to show our logo when someone drives by our restaurant. The customer can then click on the logo and get more info and a unique offer.[86]

6. Sing it to the world -- National players play national games and so goes the advertising of the largest franchisors. And honesty often works wonders to attract customers, especially if a turnaround is needed. Domino's leveraged an honest message about product quality and shared it with the nation. But what gives it more legs? When a franchisee fully executes on the national promise. From a guest post over at Repman blog by Sam Gordon:

> Last month Domino's Pizza started their Pizza Turnaround campaign, telling consumers that Domino's has heard the complaints regarding their pizza and is responding. As I'm sure you've seen, Domino's takes its campaign farther than simply advertising a new pizza. It displays real customers' most negative tweets and comments with actual Domino's chefs reacting to them.
>
> I, for one, thought this was genius and audibly gave the ad a wow the first time I saw it. One of the rare times a company actually admits its mistakes (before a giant recall or government takeover) and makes a commitment to correct the course.
>
> Knowing I had the money back guarantee in my back pocket if it was a train wreck, I picked up the phone and ordered two mediums for the first time in six years, i.e., college.

86. http://www.pmq.com/September-2016/Firenza-Pizza-uses-innovative-tools-including-Waze-and-Snapchat-to-expand-its-marketing-reach/

The result: eh.

Better? From what I recall of their pizza, yeah, it's better—especially the crust. But I'm still not a fan of their pizza.

Here is what I am a fan of though:

After my pizza experience, I took ten minutes and gave feedback on their corporate site. I received no immediate reply and thought I suppose those comments went into a database and will be ignored, or they'll just cut me a check or perhaps they are planning to film a surprise visit to me with free pizza and use it for their next commercial!

Actually, the last was not far off. A week later I received a phone call from the local Domino's franchise owner. After apologizing for the delay, she offered me a full refund, but said that she would love the chance to change my mind by sending my entire office pizza that day for lunch. She was confident if I tried a few options that I would enjoy Domino's Pizza.

Impressed with the personal touch, I was game to try and have my mind changed. She ended up sending my office five pizzas and happily accepted everyone's feedback, the positive (there was more than I expected) and the negative.

To me, this is the impressive part of Domino's campaign.

Not only is the company taking a chance and displaying some vulnerability (my ex-girlfriend would be so proud), but they are backing up their marketing efforts with good old-fashioned customer service and moderately improved pizza.

This campaign made me wonder why more companies don't take such bold measures as to admit there might, just might be something they can fix with their product (I'm looking at you AT&T Wireless Coverage, United Airlines, and Star Wars Episodes I, II and III).

Sure, after our office pizza party I still really didn't love Domino's pizza, but here's what happened when I told the franchise owner that. She offered to have me come into the store and taste all of the different options they have. She's still confident I will find something I like—I'm going in this week.

I suppose the reason that more companies don't take such bold measures is because they are unwilling to follow them up with bold actions. Bravo Domino's for trying.[87]

7. Promise of a national brand -- 7-Eleven is a well-known brand and on their franchising website, the franchisor is not shy about trumpeting their benefits. From the 7-Eleven website:

There's a reason people around the world recognize the 7-Eleven brand. It's called advertising. As a Franchisee, you reap all the rewards of some pretty incredible ad campaigns and marketing strategies. These include national TV and radio commercials, social media, special events and promotions—even public relations support. We've also got you covered on a local

87. http://www.repmanblog.com/repman/2010/02/we-suckbut-were-working-on-it.html

> level with grand opening packages, bilingual support, in-store signage and more.[88]

8. Moe's lagniappe saves the day -- An advertising promise executed by franchisees to stand out goes a long way to solidify the national brand. As noted on Yelp.com, Moe's Southwest Grill is known for free chips and salsa[89]. As a reviewer noted, "Wanted to hate this place because I figured it couldn't be as good as Chipotle. I was wrong. Food is awesome! Better choices for toppings. Free chips! Definitely my new favorite place."

9. One Down and One to Go -- It is like the gift that keeps on giving! Maggiano's Italian restaurant provides another example of franchisees executing on a national promise to deliver the brand plus the SYSTEM's intended customer delight. Taken from a tweet from @rkelly97: "At Maggiano's restaurant, if you order a classic pasta you get to pick one to take home. They bring it with the check."[90]

10. This is a no complaint zone -- Free product or service becomes a powerful apology when sincerely delivered. And freebies can work well to sample and upsell existing happy customers. Bolocco, purveyor of globally inspired burritos, leverages freebies across its franchised location for various marketing reasons, primarily to raise the value of its brand as opposed to discounting. From the online *Forbes* article written by the Young Entrepreneur Council:

> Boloco [is] a brand that deploys surprise and delight around the clock. This Boston-based restaurant chain isn't shy about offering freebies to compensate for messing up a customer's order. The company keeps

88. http://franchise.7-eleven.com/franchise/the-brand

89. https://www.yelp.cl/menu/moes-southwest-grill-wilmington-2/item/free-chips-and-salsa

90. https://twitter.com/rkelly976

an ear out for less-than-completely-satisfied feedback and bends over backwards to make things right. Is the salsa mysteriously missing from your burrito? A free menu item will be magically added onto your rewards card.

Free Burrito Days aren't anything new; the company has been doing them regularly since 2009 to show appreciation for its community and customers. Boloco's CEO, John Pepper, began hosting them based on his gut instinct that they were the right thing to do for the business. As opposed to discounts that can devalue a brand, Pepper believes "free" is a magic word. Unlike "50 percent off," "free" is truly delightful to people, compelling customers to do extraordinary things—like wait in some very long lines.

In 2012, Boloco handed out exactly 37,600 freebies (a total of $110,000 in burritos) and, as an extra good deed for the community, raised $20,717 for Life Is Good Playmakers, a nonprofit foundation of Boston-based apparel company Life Is Good.

As Pepper says, "The reason we do it is because we think Boloco is the place you can visit often enough that, over time, we can make up for the things we give away and have a good business because of it."

It's a tradeoff: giving away thousands of burritos in return for thousands of ecstatic, loyal customers.[91]

91. http://www.forbes.com/sites/theyec/2012/11/07/why-free-is-like-magic-the-roi-of-surprising-your-customers/

CHAPTER RECAP: MANAGE

Manage, according to Dictionary.com, involves "succeeding in attaining one's aims, especially against heavy odds." When Manage includes both Support and Advertising, those who execute it best will go a long way toward creating successful franchisees who achieve their dreams.

PART III

USING 3-D DEVELOPMENT

CHAPTER 11

DISCOVER

"Education is a progressive discovery of our own ignorance."

- Will Durant

Knowing where you are allows you meet yourself there, to gather the needed resources and chart a plan of improvement. So, first discover where you are. Take this self-graded assessment regarding the different links of the SYSTEM. This section more profoundly showcases the links between each area as a deficiency in one area influences another.

We have shared why each of the SYSTEM pieces is important and some of the linkages between the different components. Truly, all put together, the power of a strong SYSTEM defines 1 + 1 equaling far more than 2. Each piece compounds the others. So, if one of the links is not as strong as the others, potentially the SYSTEM could break apart. To illustrate the opportunity and the strength within the SYSTEM, we have shared several examples for each SYSTEM component to provide ideas of how some well-known franchisors are taking each piece to the next level.

Now it is your turn. It is time for an honest assessment of each component and how your franchise performs. Not to worry, no one sees this score but you and those with whom you choose to share. Transfer your scores to the scorecard on page 121 to identify what areas have the most opportunity to grow your business.

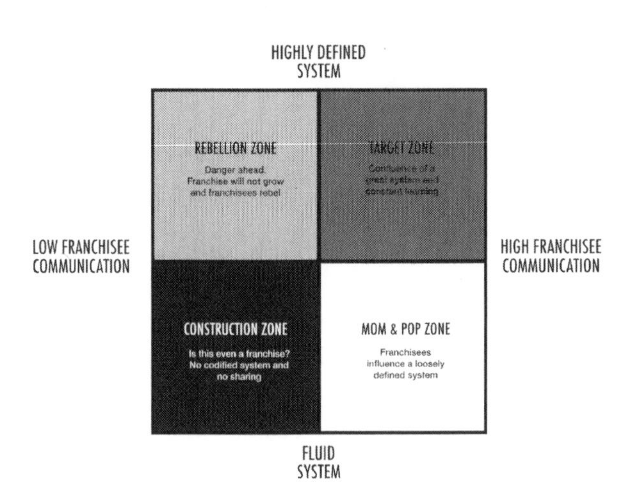

Bear in mind without the right mix of SYSTEM and franchise communication, the wheels fall off of the bus. A well codified system without listening to the franchisees and without harvesting top performer's knowledge will cause a rebellion in the franchise as the franchisee base will feel that they have invested in yet another corporate job where they are to do what they are told. On the flip side, if the franchisor tries to be everyone's friend, allowing various changes to the SYSTEM, the culture and point of difference breaks down, and it is no better than a Mom & Pop collective buying group. However, a codified SYSTEM with the right mix communication builds a strong engaged franchise base.

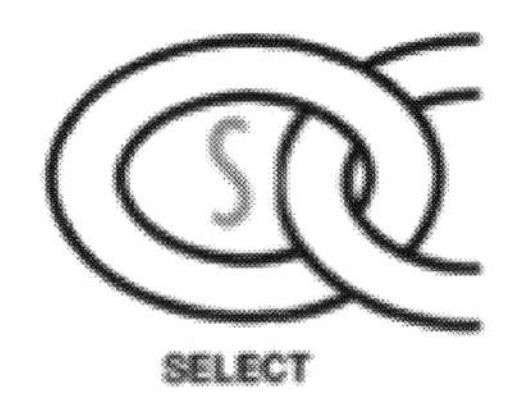

SELECTION

Selection includes using the steps necessary to discover if the prospect is a match for your franchise before inviting them to join your organization. The success of this piece is often best judged in hindsight and then tweaked to improve with insights. These questions help assess opportunities for a better selection.

1. Out of the last 10 new franchisees, how many align with your culture?

2. Out of the 10 franchisees with the longest tenure in your system, how many align with your culture?

3. Out of a sample of 10 people, how many of your Home Office employees align with your culture?

4. Out of a sample of 10 people, how many of your franchisees' employees align with your culture?

Add the numbers from 1, 2, 3, and 4. This creates your score for this section. If your score is below 34, please review the Design section under Selection.

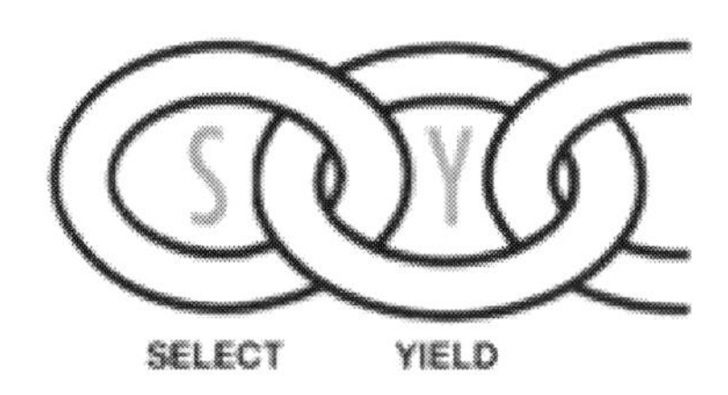

YIELD

Yield focuses on two pieces—Knowledge of the SYSTEM gathered from the founding members and top performers and then how the franchisee base Complies and Produce in order to achieve the goals of both the franchisor and franchisee. These questions help assess opportunities for acquiring and utilizing knowledge.

1. Does your SYSTEM measure and require what drives results? (Yes or No)

2. Does your SYSTEM have a formalized council that takes and utilizes feedback of top performers? (Yes or No)

3. If applicable, does your SYSTEM share knowledge across brand platforms? (Yes or No)

If you answered no to any of these questions or paused to considered if you could truthfully answer yes, then review the Yield section in the Design Chapter.

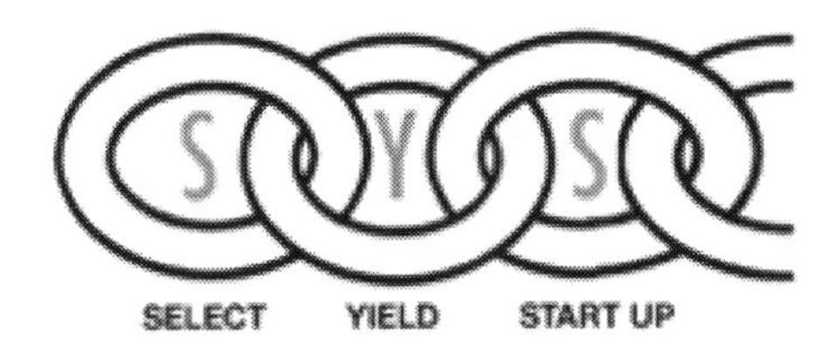

START UP

Start Up takes the right people from selecting well and equips them to sit in the driver's seat of their franchise location. This area is akin to building a strong foundation. These questions help assess opportunities for a faster track to success.

1. Do you assign pre-work before a new franchisee attends their first live training? (Yes or No)

2. Do you assign financial coaches to each new franchisee to ensure their understanding of the financials? (Yes or No)

3. Does the training involve demonstration followed by verification through action that the franchisee understands the lesson? (Yes or No)

4. Do you assign franchisee mentors in some fashion to new franchisees, including apprenticeships or other structures? (Yes or No)

If you answered no to any of these questions or paused to considered if you could truthfully answer yes, then review the Start Up section in the Design Chapter.

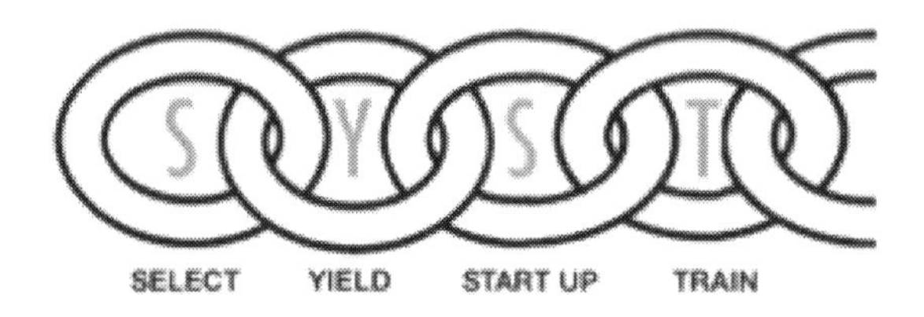

TRAINING

This area covers the ability to receive Knowledge as well as the ability to Comply and Produce. Educating across the franchise base from new to mature franchisees, in addition to those franchisees with various backgrounds and experiences. These questions help discern areas for improvement in training.

1. Out of a sample of 10 people, how many of your franchisee base attend regular trainings?

2. Out of a sample of 10 trainings, how many of your trainings introduce newly acquired knowledge to further the business vs. advancement of existing tools and concepts?

3. Out of a sample of 10 trainings, how many of your trainings are specialized- special topics or customized by the franchisee background or length of time in the SYSTEM?

Add the numbers from 1, 2, 3. This creates your score for this section. If your score is below 21, then please review the section under Training.

ENGAGE

Culture drives whom you select as a franchisee, the point of difference that attracts and retains customers as well as fosters franchisee engagement. These questions dig at the heart of Engagement and Culture.

1. Out of a sample of 10 people, how many of your franchisee base attend meetings each year?

2. Out of a sample of 10 people, how many of your franchisees could accurately answer this question: "What are you paid to do?"

Add the numbers from 1, 2. This creates your score for this section. If your score is below 15, then please review the Engagement and Culture section.

MANAGE

Manage covers how a franchisor supports the franchise base and what tools it makes available to acquire, delight, and retain customers. These questions focus on the franchisor's support level as an in-

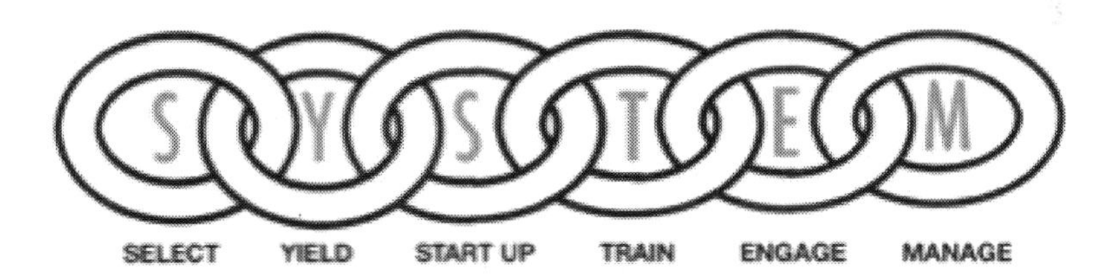

dicator of helping the franchisee follow the SYSTEM that attracts, delights, and retains customers.

1. Out of a sample of 10 people, how many of your field support staff can name the goals of the franchisees that they support? This is an indicator of their relationship and 'earn money' is not

specific enough. The answer should contain the amount desired and how it will improve the franchise's life or some goal that is more specific than 'support the family,' 'earn more money,' and similar statements.

2. Out of a sample of 10 people, how many of your franchisees would say that the franchisor "has their back"?

3. Out of a sample of 10 people, how many of your franchisees would describe their relationship with the franchisor as a partnership?

4. Out of a sample of 10 people, how many of your support staff visit their franchisees' locations annually?

Add the numbers from 1, 2, 3, and 4. This creates your score for this section. If your score is below 32, then please review the Manage section.

If any part of Advertising - acquiring, delighting, or retaining customers - holds an opportunity, then thoroughly review the next sections regarding the Five R.U.L.E.S. of Purple Goldfish and 12 Types of Purple Goldfish for ideas about how to create customers who love your passion and points of differentiation.

SCORECARD

Track your answers here to more easily identify opportunities to improve.

SELECTION	QUESTIONS	ANSWER (1-10)	GOAL SCORE
Question #1	Out of the last 10 new franchisees, how many align with your culture?		
Question #2	Out of the 10 franchisees with the longest tenure in your system, how many align with your culture?		
Question #3	Out of a sample of 10 people, how many of your Home Office employees align with your culture?		
Question #4	Out of a sample of 10 people, how many of your franchisees' employees align with your culture?		
TOTAL			34+

YIELD	QUESTIONS	ANSWER (YES OR NO)	GOAL SCORE
Question #1	Does your SYSTEM measure and require what drive results?		
Question #2	Does your SYSTEM have a formalized council that takes and utilizes feedback of top performers?		
Question #3	Does your SYSTEM share knowledge across brand platforms?		
TOTAL			Address NO's

START UP	QUESTIONS	ANSWER (YES OR NO)	GOAL SCORE
Question #1	Do you assign pre-work before a new franchisee attends their first live training?		
Question #2	Do you assign financial coaches to each new franchisee to ensure their understanding of the financials?		
Question #3	Does the training involve demonstration followed by verification, so the franchisee understands the lesson?		
Question #4	Do you assign franchisee mentors in some fashion to new franchisees, including apprenticeships or other structures?		
TOTAL			Address NO's

TRAINING	QUESTIONS	ANSWER (1-10)	GOAL SCORE
Question #1	Out of a sample of 10 people, how many of your franchisee base attend regular trainings?		
Question #2	Out of a sample of 10 trainings, how many of your trainings introduce newly acquired knowledge to further the business vs. advancement of existing tools and concepts?		
Question #3	Out of a sample of 10 trainings, how many of your trainings are specialized topics or customized based on franchisee background or length of time in the SYSTEM?		
TOTAL			21+

ENGAGEMENT	QUESTIONS	ANSWER (1-10)	GOAL SCORE
Question #1	Out of a sample of 10 people, how many of your franchisee base attend meetings each year?		
Question #2	Out of a sample of 10 people, how many of your franchisees could accurately answer this question, "What are you paid to do?"		
TOTAL			16+

MANAGE	QUESTIONS	ANSWER (1-10)	GOAL SCORE
Question #1	Out of a sample of 10 people, how many of your field support staff can name the goals of the franchisees they support?		
Question #2	Out of a sample of 10 people, how many of your franchisees would say the franchisor "has their back?"		
Question #3	Out of a sample of 10 people, how many of your franchisees would describe their relationship with the franchisor as a partnership?		
Question #4	Out of a sample of 10 people, how many of your support staff visit their franchisees locations annually?		
TOTAL			32+

CHAPTER 12

DESIGN

"Design is a plan for arranging elements in such a way as best to accomplish a particular purpose."

- Charles Eames

Knowing what you need is often half the battle. So now that you have assessed areas where you wish to grow, it is time to put together a plan to acquire the tools needed and then implement. In Design, peel the onion layer by layer to assess the area that will benefit most from attention. Peeling back the onion involves asking question after question until you hit the crux of the matter. Remember, these are not issues or problems but rather opportunities to grow.

Two heads are better than one. Discuss the areas that you wish to improve across the Home Office as well as with your Advisory Board(s) and/or top performers. This may provide a bigger picture of the opportunity so that fullness of the opportunity and plan are captured. Furthermore, franchisees want to contribute to the solution, so it goes a long way when one franchisee shares their excitement and ownership of improvement with a colleague, as a top down push alienates. Many franchisees escaped the corporate world just to avoid top down pushes.

We will recommend a few areas to review depending upon how you scored your franchise. Consider these tips as you design a plan:

1. Research!

- Get feedback from key stakeholders, which may include third party partners.
    - Consider quick online surveys to gather additional input
    - Consider contacting your franchise customer base directly for input
- Stick to the facts. It is easy to apply conjecture, but the facts will lead to an impactful outcome.

- Study key competitors and determine if your points of differentiation are as strong as ever. Consider a Strength, Weakness, Opportunity, and Threat analysis.

2. Where Do I Want to Go? How will changes in one section change other pieces of the SYSTEM and will this build a stronger path to your 3, 5, and 10-year vision?

3. Write it Down! A recent *Forbes* article by Marc Murphy, Contributor, shares that "vividly describing your goals in written form is strongly associated with goal success, and people who very vividly describe or picture their goals are anywhere from 1.2 to 1.4 times more likely to successfully accomplish their goals than people who don't."[92]

4. Document What You Want to Achieve. Understand how you will achieve it and what will measure it. If it isn't measured, then it did not happen.

5. Test, Aim, Fire. Select a subset to test first and then learn, adjust, and deploy.

6. Determine the WII-FM. Make certain that all stakeholders know "what is in it for me." As you design, make certain that all stakeholders have a why.

SELECTION

Within Selection, what is at the root of the opportunity? Is it the salesforce being unclear on your culture and what you seek in a franchisee? If so, then take a look at the examples where the franchisor puts their culture on display. Review the examples where those who do not operate within the culture are called out for correction.

---

92. https://www.forbes.com/sites/markmurphy/2018/04/15/neuroscience-explains-why-you-need-to-write-down-your-goals-if-you-actually-want-to-achieve-them/#88fd79f79059

Or does the opportunity stem from adding what looks like Ferraris but turn out to be 4-cylinder cars to your franchise? If so, what could you learn from the pre-testing and homework examples that would aid in course correction?

YIELD

Issues in this area arise when there are too many measures to follow or many measures have only an indirect impact on results. Or perhaps the tools to measure the indicators are hard to find or apply inconsistent definitions so that comparing apples to apples is a mystery.

Do you have a way of collecting, documenting, and implementing feedback from top performers? If these top guns are open to giving feedback, then examine how you can capture their recommendations and learning. Have you thoroughly captured the entire point, avoiding omission of something that may seem trivial but in fact may not be? Have you avoided omissions that are uncomfortable for some to hear? It is one thing to capture well the top performer knowledge but that knowledge benefits no one unless it is harnessed and put to work across the SYSTEM.

So, examine how you implement the Knowledge and, of course, how you measure the idea once implemented, so that you can tweak and continue to grow. The implementation piece may have opportunity in the way training is presented. However, if top performers are quiet, then culture may house the opportunity.

START UP

To repair this section, start with your lowest score. Then go to the Start Up section and look for examples that apply.

Is pre-work missing, leaving new franchisees with their heads spinning after training?

Is it a lack of a mentorship program? If so, then see the mentor and apprenticeship examples.

Is there an opportunity to take the example of making support an honor and upgrading your training talent? If so, examine some of the hands-on examples from that section.

TRAINING

Are trainings highly anticipated and attended? If not, assess.

Are we training on the right topics that connect to meaningful KPI that deliver customer delight time and time again?

Are we communicating the 'What Is In It For Me?' with each training opportunity?

Are trainings meeting franchisees where they are?

Is there pre-training to help franchisees digest the live message?

Have you deployed a version of hands on training?

Does the training message align across your SYSTEM- in Mission, Vision, Culture and Goals?

Answers to opportunities in this area not only come from the Training examples, but are impacted by the Selection of Franchisees and the Culture of the organization. Fostering a culture of continued growth aid in robust training attendance.

ENGAGEMENT AND CULTURE

Is the opportunity pervasive? Has the Home Office abandoned the intended culture?

Or is there a segment—say the franchisees who have been around for a while—who have left the culture and lack engagement? If so, seek the examples where everyone holds each other accountable.

If the percentage of those attending trainings and meetings is low, examine franchisors who harvest and implement knowledge from the top performers. It is easy to ask a franchise advisory council to share their thoughts on why attendance is low. If it is a matter of the team not knowing how they earn their money (living the mission and executing the SYSTEM), then look at some of the training best practices to communicate the message.

MANAGE

The Support team should be the cream that rises to the top. If this is not the case, then examine what skills are missing. Consider cross training with top performers and look for the best to staff this area.

Is it that you have the best, but the ratio of franchisees to support staff is too high? If so, look to adjust the number of people per support team member.

With Advertising, is there a pain point that the average franchise struggles to overcome in the customer experience cycle? If so, look at some of the examples where franchisors take the pain point and make it a done-for-you service by the Home Office.

DESIGN SUMMARY

"The first step in solving a problem is to recognize that it does exist."- Zig Ziglar

Kudos for taking the hardest step to taking advantage of an opportunity – admitting that you have an opportunity to solve. As author John Maxwell shares in his book, Developing the Leader Within You, problems are opportunities. So, you have recognized an opportunity to grow your business, improve unit economics for your strategic partners, the franchisees, and you are starting a journey continual growth. As the saying goes, "If you always do what you've always done, you'll always get what you've always got."

And in some cases, if the competition is evolving and you sit still doing what you have always done, then you will actually achieve less and less and the competition advances. The only way to achieve more is to capture the opportunity. A business colleague quotes the poet Marshall Mathers in these situations. As Mathers, whose stage name is Eminem, states, "Look, if you had one shot, one opportunity, to seize everything you ever wanted, One moment, Would you capture it or just let it slip?"

So, kudos for taking the step to capture your opportunity!

CHAPTER 13

DEPLOY

"The single biggest problem in communication is the illusion that it has taken place."

-George Bernard Shaw

Deploying the plan requires communication to all involved parties in a way that all parties understand the big five questions as applicable: who, what, why, when, where. Based upon franchise examples, the following tips may aid in successfully implementing your designed plan:

- **Match the Mission and Culture** - How does the designed plan match your current mission? How does it align with the culture as well as the short-term and long-term plan?

- **Use Top Training Tips** - Make sure that the message makes sense to all of your franchisees—meeting them where they are at this moment and providing a way for them to translate it to their employees.

- **Advisory Board** - Use an Advisory Board to provide input and play an important role in communicating the plan to constituents. This will increase engagement and two heads are always better than one.

- **Test, Perfect, Deploy!** - Especially in larger franchises, consider testing with a subset of the franchisees to gain faster feedback and to work out any kinks in the plan before a larger rollout.

- **Track** - Make sure that the new plan has Yield and Comply components and a way to communicate the improvement (or not) to the franchise base.

- **Implement** – Carry out the updates across trainings as applicable, from start up through existing franchisee trainings.

PART IV

CLOSING

CHAPTER 14

LAGNIAPPE: THE NEW FRANCHISE HORIZON

"Adaptabiity is about the powerful difference between adapting to cope and adapting to win."

- Max McKeow

In the 2010s, the Gig Economy arose. Since 2009, 1099 self-employment forms have increased 22 percent.[93] In 2016, according to Pew Research, 24 percent of Americans report earnings from the digital platform economy.[94] This platform includes earning money for a job or task as well as selling items online.

Many of the Gig Economy workers rely on an App to secure a job. Under this set of Gig jobs, Uber and Lyft come immediately to mind. Many others exist too. A Wonolo blog post[95] by Angela Stringfellow shares top apps. A sample of them includes:

- AirBNB - rent your home to travelers for various periods of time
- Amazon Flex -workers choose opportunities for pay between $18 - $25
- Bellhops - aid with DIY moving
- Care.com - seniors, kids, and dogs
- Closet Collective - rent your designer clothes
- Fancy Hands - apply for assistant gigs
- Grubhub - food delivery
- Handy - handymen and cleaners
- HelloTech - help customers with technology
- InstaCart - deliver groceries

93. https://www.forbes.com/sites/gregoryferenstein/2015/12/12/the-gig-economy-appears-to-be-growing-heres-why/
94. http://www.pewinternet.org/2016/11/17/gig-work-online-selling-and-home-sharing/
95. https://www.wonolo.com/blog/best-gig-economy-apps/

- Roadie - pick up and drop off things
- Shipt - deliver groceries
- Taki - handyman, cleaning, or hauling services
- TaskEasy - affordable lawn care
- YourMechanic - a mechanic that makes house calls
- Zeel- massage therapist

So, what does this have to do with a franchise? Well, it is a business with entrepreneurs offering specified services/goods for customers, sharing a common brand, common operating system, and the app owner and gig worker form a partnership to acquire, delight, and retain customers.

Is this the next evolution of franchising? Perhaps it will inspire new twists and new opportunities for franchisors as franchises must evolve to their ever-changing world. Perhaps it will add opportunities for conversions. If your franchise competes in a Gig Economy area, then perhaps some will want to own a business where they can multiple revenue by hiring others and will need/benefit from that SYSTEM from a franchisor. Or perhaps the gig experience will prepare more employees for a job with your franchisees to have a face as an employer vs. a digital brand.

CHAPTER 15

TOP FIVE TAKEAWAYS

"Advice is like a tablet of aspirin.
It only works if you actually take it."

- David Murphy

Here are the top five takeaways from *Purple Goldfish Franchise Edition*:

1. Culture is Everything. It is the glue that binds franchisees to each other as well as to the franchisor. Executed throughout all pieces of the SYSTEM, it differentiates the customer experience, guides how customer opportunities are handled and shapes the partnership between franchisor and franchisee.

2. Build the House. Start Up must provide that great foundation, and it cannot be built in a one-shot week program. It must come in chunks across a period of time for absorption.

3. Harvest Your Crop. Make sure to connect franchisees to each other as well as to corporate to grow your knowledge base. Then bundle your harvest and take it to market—package the knowledge and disseminate it to the SYSTEM.

4. Support the Family. Make sure that field support has the right ratio of franchisees to support staff and that support folks are top of their field and carry a shared accountability with the franchisee for results.

5. Communicate. With an ever-changing marketplace and many franchise options as well as DIY, communicating who you are—what you know, how to best deploy the SYSTEM knowledge as well as improve it, track it and grow it—will lead to where you wish to go.

PART V

BONUS

CHAPTER 16

POWERED BY GIFT ECONOMY PRINCIPLES

"There are two types of economies. In a commodity (or exchange) economy, status is accorded to those who have the most. In a gift economy, status is accorded to those who give the most to others."

- Lewis Hyde

EXPLORING THE IDEAS OF SURPLUS OR STATUS

We're fascinated by the concept of a "gift economy" and how it relates to providing a Purple Goldfish. If you've never heard of the gift economy, it's a social science principle that states valuable goods and services are regularly given without explicit agreement for immediate or future rewards. In a perfect world, simultaneous or recurring giving serves to circulate and redistribute valuables within a society. Put another way, it's the principle of reciprocity in motion.

A gift economy is the opposite of a market economy. In a market economy, there is an exact exchange of values (quid pro quo). It is our theory, there is a hybrid called the lagniappe economy that can sit between the gift and market economies.

Here is a great analysis from a post by Kevin von Duuglas-ittu on gift economies:

> This does not mean that the Gift Economy and the Market Economy of business are incompatible, not in the least. In fact, many, if not most, of our business exchanges are grounded in giftbased relationships whose "gift" nature we simply are unconscious of and just assume. If you develop a keen eye for the giftgiving environment and think about all the things that gift giving in those environments signal: (1) A surplus others want to attach themselves to, (2) A magnanimous respect for the relationship beyond all else, (3) A debt structure that is positive.[96]

Let's examine each of the three environments through the lens of a lagniappe economy:

---

96. https://socialmediamediasres.wordpress.com/2011/02/16/social-media-is-like-beer-buying-the-gift-economy-in-social-media/

1. **Surplus** – The idea of surplus is grounded in giving extra or creating an inequality. Lagniappe is the practice by the business of throwing in little extras at the time of purchase.

2. **Respect** – The gift or little extra is about respect for the relationship. It becomes a beacon, a sign that shows you care. It's a physical sign of goodwill and customer appreciation.

3. **Positive** – A debt structure that is positive. This speaks to exceeding expectations by giving extra. The idea of an equal exchange (market exchange) is a myth in marketing. You either exceed or fall short of customer expectations. Providing that extra value provides an inequality that is positive. The positive effect leads to a sort of indebtedness or reciprocity on behalf of the customer. The benefit of surplus is status

As a business, why would you want to incorporate gift economy principles into your market exchanges? We believe that there are three distinct reasons and corresponding benefits of the status gained through providing a lagniappe:

1. **Positioning** – Stand out from your competition. If everyone is providing "x," the fact that you provide x + y (gift) then differentiates your offering. Less than 30% of consumers buy on price. You want to tap into the 70+% who are looking for value and a strong customer experience. Benefit: Differentiation

2. **Loyalty** – Giving the little extra (gift) enhances the customer experience. It creates a bond between the business and the customer. The benefits of that bond include increased loyalty and ultimately patronage as a form of repayment. Benefit: Retention

3. **Reciprocity** – Part of giving extra is to create goodwill (inequality). That inequality is repaid by positive word of mouth or digital word of mouse. The best form of marketing is via positive word

of mouth. By giving a signature extra (gift) you provide something for your customers to talk, tweet, blog, Yelp, or post to Facebook about. Benefit: Referrals

THE POWER OF A CHOCOLATE CHIP COOKIE

The chocolate chip cookie was a thread throughout the original Purple Goldfish Project where Stan set out to collect 1,001 examples. DoubleTree and their signature chocolate chip cookie was cited so many times that DoubleTree became the first brand inducted into the Purple Goldfish Hall of Fame. The hotel has built a reputation on a unique treat that keeps leisure and business travelers coming back for more: its legendary chocolate chip cookie presented to each guest at check-in.

Here are a few fun facts about the legendary cookie:

- DoubleTree gives out approximately 60,000 chocolate chip cookies each day. That's more than twenty million each year!

- DoubleTree began giving out chocolate chip cookies in the early 1980s, when many hotels across the country used them as treats for VIPs.

- In 1995, DoubleTree enlisted the services of Nashville based Christie Cookie Company to hold the brand's secret recipe, which ensures that the same, delicious cookie is delivered consistently at every DoubleTree property.

- Every DoubleTree chocolate chip cookie is baked fresh daily at each hotel.

- Each cookie weighs more than 2 ounces and has an average of 20 chocolate chips.

- The Christie Cookie Company uses more than 580,000 pounds of chocolate chips each year for DoubleTree's cookies.
- To date, more than 300,000,000 cookies have been served to delighted guests and customers.
- More than one million chocolate chip cookies have been donated by DoubleTree hotels to celebrate and thank deserving members of the community from doctors and nurses to police and firefighters, as well as nonprofit groups such as orphanages, food banks and homeless shelters.[97]

What's so special about a cookie?

DoubleTree offers an explanation right on the brown paper bag the cookie comes in. "Why a cookie?" the headline asks. "Cookies are warm, personal and inviting, much like our hotels and the staff here that serves you." In a recent *New York Times* article, a Vivaldi Partners executive, Erich Joachimsthaler, said, "When consumers don't know how to judge the benefits or the differentiation of a product—I don't know the difference between Midwest and JetBlue and United—then a meaningless attribute like cookies can create meaningful differentiation… . The giveaway creates buzz, it creates differentiation, it increases a purchase decision."

We don't necessarily agree with the word "meaningless," especially if that little extra is a signature element. We subscribe to the philosophy that Malcolm Gladwell offered in *The Tipping Point,* "The little things can make the biggest difference." The chocolate chip cookie is not just a chocolate chip cookie. It's much more than that.

The value of a satisfied customer to a business is immense. One study showed that customers who are totally satisfied contribute 17 times more sales to a firm than customers who are somewhat

---

97. http://www.doubletreecookies.com/the_cookie_history

dissatisfied and 2.6 times more sales than customers who are somewhat satisfied. If all it takes to improve attitudes of customers is an appreciatory comment and an occasional gift, then organizations should use this approach as part of their marketing strategies.

PEANUTS WHILE YOU WAIT

Another member of the Purple Goldfish "Hall of Fame" is Five Guys Burgers and Fries. Founder, Jerry Murrell, and his eponymous five sons represent the principles of a lagniappe. For background, Matt and Jim travel the country visiting stores, Chad oversees training, Ben selects the franchisees, and Tyler runs the bakery.

Added value is baked into the model at Five Guys:

1. Free peanuts when you walk through the door
2. 15 free toppings for your hamburger or hot dog
3. Free refills for your soda or ice tea
4. The building is free of logos and excess décor

The free peanuts that you can shell are our favorite. While you wait for your order to be prepared, there is a mountain of peanuts just inside the front door to munch on. Free peanuts have become the trademark "thing" that Five Guys is known for. Next to the door, you'll often see over fifty bags, 50 pounds apiece, waiting to be opened and devoured. Overall, it's a pretty cool thing: order your cheeseburger and scarf down a handful of salty, ballparkstyle, stillintheshell peanuts.

By our rough calculations, Five Guys gives away over five million pounds of peanuts per year. Do little things make a big difference? For a company that does little to no advertising, we would certainly say so. The mantra from Jerry Murrell is, "We figure that our best salesman is our customer. Treat that person right, he'll walk out the door and sell for you. From the beginning, I wanted people to know that we put all our money into the food."[98]

98. http://www.inc.com/magazine/20100401/jerrymurrellfiveguysburgersandfries.html

CHAPTER 17

THE FIVE INGREDIENTS OR R.U.L.E.S. OF A PURPLE GOLDFISH

"Existence is no more than the precarious attainment of relevance in an intensely mobile flux of past, present, and future."

- Susan Sontag

MAKING LAGNIAPPE IS LIKE MAKING JAMBALAYA

Have you ever made jambalaya from scratch? It's a bunch of different ingredients all thrown in together where the chef takes a look at what's laying around in the kitchen and throws it all into a pot. Let your concoction stew with some spices thrown in and...voilà! You have a yourself a jambalaya or a Purple Goldfish for this example's sake. Here are the five main ingredients of our jambalaya or, if you are an acronym fan like we are, the R.U.L.E.S.

1. **Relevant** – The item or benefit should be of value to the recipient.

2. **Unexpected** – The extra benefit or gift should be a surprise. It is something thrown in for good measure.

3. **Limited** – If it's a small token or gift, it has to be rare, hard to find, or unique to your business.

4. **Expression** – Many times it comes down to the gesture. It becomes more about "how" it is given, as opposed to "what" is given.

5. **Sticky** – Is it memorable enough that the person will want to share their experience by telling a friend or everyone that they know about it?

FIRST INGREDIENT: RELEVANT

The first rule, and probably the most important ingredient for a Purple Goldfish, is relevancy. If it's just a throw-in or SWAG (stuff we all get), then the gift is probably not that relevant. It needs to be a gift that is actually valued by your customer.

SECOND INGREDIENT: UNEXPECTED

Steve Knox of Tremor, a P&G agency, wrote an enlightened post in *Ad Age* entitled, "Why Effective Word of Mouth Disrupts Schemas." The article explains how to leverage cognitive disruption to drive word of mouth. When they receive something unexpected, people feel compelled or even "forced" to talk about the experience.

First off, let us admit that we had no clue what a "schema" was. Here is our interpretation of the word. It turns out that our brain remains typically in a static state. It relies on developing cognitive schemas to figure out how the world works. It recognizes patterns and adapts behavior accordingly. Your brain basically doesn't want to have to think.

For example, every day you get into the car and you know instinctively to drive on the right side of the road. Fast forward and you're on a trip to the UK or Australia. The first time you drive on the left side, it throws you through a loop. It's disruptive to your normal driving schema and it forces the brain to think, which thereby elicits discussion (i.e. word of mouth).

Steve also provided some great examples in his article. Our favorite example was for a new Secret deodorant product that P&G was launching which featured a deodorant that utilized a moisture activated ingredient that kicked in when you sweat. The brand understood that this could be positioned against a traditional schema which was understood by their focus groups that stated, "the more you work out, the more you sweat, and the worse you smell." Ultimately, the tagline for the brand became, "The More You Move, the Better You Smell." A staggering 51,000 consumers posted comments on P&G's website about the product.

Stan started thinking how this idea of disruption applies to the concept of a lagniappe. The second ingredient in the lagniappe

R.U.L.E.S. is the concept of being "unexpected." It's that little something that's an unexpected extra at the time of purchase. It's the unexpected surprise and delight that triggers disruption of our schemas.

Let's face it—most companies fail to deliver an exceptional customer experience. It's only when a brand does anything to go above and beyond that we get shocked. And what happens when we receive that unexpected lagniappe act of kindness? We tell our friends, we tweet it, and we post to Facebook about it. Those are the only types of positive experiences that are amplified.

THIRD INGREDIENT: LIMITED

The third of the R.U.L.E.S. is the concept of being "limited." What does limited mean? If it's a small token or extra, it means selecting something unique to your business. Ideally you want it to be signature to your brand. Something rare, different, or just plain hard to find elsewhere. A limited extra helps you differentiate your offering(s), while providing insurance against being copied by competitors.

FOURTH INGREDIENT: EXPRESSION

The fourth of the R.U.L.E.S. is "expression." Expression speaks to "*how you give*" as opposed to "*what you give.*" A Purple Goldfish is a beacon. It's a sign that shows you care. That little extra touch demonstrates that the customer matters.

One of the signature elements of staying in a state room on a Carnival Cruise is the towel animals. Every night, guests return to their room to find one of the 40 different types of animals. A cruise favorite, the folks at Carnival create about seven million towel animals per year. Suffice to say, that's a lot of folding!

Several years ago, Carnival released a book called *Carnival Towel Creations.* The 88 pages encompass a "how to" manual on towel animal making. Think it's easy? New stewards at Carnival spend at least 10 hours of formal training to master the art of the fold. One of the things that we like about the towel animals is how Carnival has leveraged them across their various touch points. They've been the focus of advertising, PR, direct mail, and are even seen online. In other words, these towel animals literally have "legs."

FIFTH INGREDIENT: STICKY

The fifth of the R.U.L.E.S. is the concept of being "sticky." You want an experience that "sticks" in the mind of consumers and promotes word of mouth. Ultimately, you want to create experiences and provide services that are both memorable and remarkable (thus worth talking about). Here are two questions to ask yourself about a proposed idea:

1. Is it water cooler material?

2. Will your customer tell three people or 3,000?

CHAPTER 18

12 TYPES OF PURPLE GOLDFISH

"There are no traffic jams along the extra mile."

-Roger Staubach

ARE YOU DOING THE LITTLE THINGS?

Giving Little Unexpected Extras (GLUE) shows that you genuinely care about the franchisees and customers that you serve. There are a dozen different types of Purple Goldfish that can be provided as a lagniappe. Half are based on "value" and half are based on "maintenance" according to the value/maintenance matrix. Think of value as the enhancement of the experience and maintenance as the support of an ongoing relationship. Here are the main elements of both:

Value (the "what" and "when" of customer experience):

- What are the benefits of your service or product to customers/franchisees?
- Does your offering go above and beyond to exceed customer/franchisee expectations?
- Are you giving that little unexpected extra to surprise and delight your customer/franchisee?

Maintenance (the "who" and "how" of customer experience):

- What is the buying experience like for your customer?
- Do you make things turnkey or simple for your customer?
- Are you responsive to problems / issues for your customer?

THE 12 TYPES OF PURPLE GOLDFISH

1. Throw-ins (value) – Little extras that are included with your product or service. They help you go beyond the transaction and stand out in a sea of sameness.

Example: Zane's Cycles

The etymology of lagniappe stems from the Quechan "yapay" which means "to give more." Zane's Cycles of Branford, Connecticut, lives by this mantra and leverages customer service as point of differentiation. A more than thirty-year veteran of the retail bicycle industry, Chris Zane has built Zane's into one of the largest bicycle stores in the nation by giving customers more than they expect. More importantly, Zane's stands behind the sale by giving more service than is reasonably expected (especially by competitors).

Zane's is willing to spend $100 to service a customer. To illustrate the point, Chris uses the metaphor of a bowl filled with 400 quarters. During presentations, he walks around with a bowl and encourages members of the audience to take quarters. Most only take a few quarters. No one ever takes the whole bowl.

According to Chris, "The point is that when you as a customer are presented with more than what seems reasonable, like a bowl of 400 quarters, you will selfregulate. By providing more service than what folks consider reasonable, we can build trust and loyalty and remind them how hard we're working on their behalf."

Here are some of the compelling ways that Zane's offers little extras to maximize lifetime value:

- **Free Trade-In Program for Kids** Buy a bike for your child at Zane's. When they outgrow it, simply bring it back to tradeup.

Zane's gives you a credit for the price of the former bike toward a new one.

- **Gift Certificates in Water Bottles** Buy a gift certificate and Zane's will throw in a complimentary branded water bottle that holds the certificate. Simple but effective.
- **The One Dollar Rule** Zane's doesn't charge for any parts that cost them one dollar or less. Need a master link for your chain? It's on the house. In fact, they typically will throw in an extra master link as a lagniappe.
- **Coffee Bar** Zane's has an awesome espresso bar in the store, encouraging customers to sit down, relax, and enjoy a cup of gourmet coffee.
- **Set of Small Tools** Zane's provides a complimentary toolkit when shipping bikes to premium recipients.
- **Webcam** Zane's has a camera in the repair shop that gives customers the ability to Skype with the repair team.
- **Personal Notes** Each person who buys a bike receives a handwritten thank you note.
- **Test Rides** Want to test a bike at Zane's? You're free to take it out for a ride. No credit card or driver's license required. Each year they lose a handful of bikes, but the small cost is insignificant compared to the trust gained when hassle has been avoided.

2. In the Bag / Out of the Box (value) - Little unexpected things that are added "in the bag" or "out of the box" as a surprise to delight consumers.

Example: Five Guys Burgers & Fries

As we discussed earlier, Five Guys has instituted a number of Purple Goldfish into their business model. The lagniappe that appears to get the most attention are the extra fries that Five Guys dumps on top of your order and subsequently all over the inside of your brown paper bag with togo orders. "Bag fries" as they've come to be known have garnered a ton of attention and differentiate Five Guys from every other fast food burger joint in town. Steve Strauss, from theselfemployed.com, had an interesting take and analysis of the Five Guys "bag fries" and recently said:

> Here's what they do: When you order some fries from the counter, the server dutifully takes their little paper fries bucket, fills it up, and then puts it in a paper bag. Then they take an even bigger scoop of fries and dump it into the bag, on top of the regular order. I always think, and my kids always say, "I can't believe how many extra fries we get!"
>
> And then it finally dawned on me, we don't really get any extra fries at all, do we? The genius of this little show is that for all intents and purposes, it looks and feels like we get extra fries, that the guys and gals at Five Guys are being cool and generous, but upon a little postcarb reflection, the truth is that they planned on giving that number of fries out anyway, and budget for that.[99]

Steve presents an interesting point, and he's right, Five Guys does budget for the fries that are being "given away." If you recall from our analysis of Five Guys earlier, by and large, owner Jerry Murrell does not believe in advertising. Instead, Murrell prefers to give a

99. https://www.theselfemployed.com/content-marketing/the-5-guys-fries-trick-that-will-blow-your-mind-and-sales/

little extra to get customers to talk about the company. However, just because you're providing a lagniappe does not mean that it has to be a cost that is not accounted for. Ultimately, Five Guys has essentially created a gift that is a fiscally responsible lagniappe and simultaneously perpetuates word of mouth advertising.

3. Sampling (value) - Give your customer an additional taste by offering a free something extra on the house. There may not be a more cost-effective way for brands to drive purchase intent and conversion than sampling. The proof is in the numbers as highlighted in this article in Brandweek. Here are the top two takeaways from the Arbitron survey: 24% of consumers bought the product they sampled instead of the item they initially set out to purchase. 35% of customers who tried a sample bought the product during the same shopping trip. But why does sampling just have to be about the prospect? Why can't you leverage current customers with an additional little extra to increase satisfaction, drive retention, and promote word of mouth?

Example: Izzy's Ice Cream

Izzy's Ice Cream is an iconic ice cream store in St. Paul. The owner, Jeff Sommers, was told to do two things when he opened his shop:

1. Smile

2. Give away samples.

Jeff disliked the idea of just giving away free samples, so he created his own wrinkle. Customers are allowed to add an "IZZY" scoop with each scoop purchased. It's a small scoop of any flavor that goes right on top of the scoop that they bought. This tactic is great for customers who can now take a "worry free" chance to try a new flavor. It's a little extra that goes a long way. Don't take our word for it. Izzy's was voted the best ice cream shop in America by *Reader's Digest.*

4. First & Last Impressions (value) - You have two chances to make an impression. When your customer comes through the door and right before they walk out, hang up, or log off. Little extras offered at these times make you memorable, and more importantly, talkable.

One of the foundations of the lagniappe is the idea of leveraging primacy and recency.[100] As an example, you've probably heard the fact that people tend to remember the first thing and the last thing they see. A ton of attention is paid to the importance of a first impression (primacy), but little is made of the last moment (recency).

The concept of doing a little unexpected extra at the time of purchase is a recency strategy. This is partly explained by Nobel Prize Winner Daniel Kahneman as the "Peak-End Rule." Kahneman believes that we judge our past experiences almost entirely on how they were at their peak (whether pleasant or unpleasant) and how they ended.

According to *Forbes* columnist, Dean Crutchfield, "Designing for the Peak-End Rule is another way of not focusing on what is less important, but about focusing on what brings the most value to the customer experience. In other words, make sure that your peak and end are memorable, branded, and differentiated."

You never get a second chance to make a first or last impression. In essence, you need give the customer something to talk, tweet, blog, Yelp, or post on Facebook right before they leave, hang up, or log out.

---

100. http://psycnet.apa.org/journals/abn/59/1/1

Example: Hard Rock Hotel

The Hard Rock Hotel in Chicago, Illinois, has gone out of its way to make its guests feel welcome. Their signature greeting lies within their "Sound of Your Stay" program[101] where the hotel will allow guests to rent a turntable or Fender guitar. There might be a $500 deposit but that does not deter guests who are elated with the unique offering. According to one reviewer on TripAdvisor, "You can rent a Fender or mixing table for free which is really cool but on top of it all, expect friendly smiles and quick service."

5. Guarantees (value) Give your customers that little extra pledge that you'll stand behind your product or service.

Example: Sheetz

Most would say that Sheetz is a gas station/convenience store, but Sheetz actually defines themselves as, "An American restaurant company with a focus on kicked-up convenience." One of Sheetz's differentiators is their promise to buy a cup of coffee for any guest that sees a blinking light on one of their coffee brewers (signifying that the coffee needs to be changed). This tactic is brilliant since consumers know that without the blinking light, the coffee is fresh. This solid guarantee helps set Sheetz apart from the competition.

6. Pay it Forward (value) Give a little extra back to the community.

Example: Mission BBQ

Business partners, Steve "Newt" Newton and Bill Kraus, set out to create a chain of barbeque restaurants that not only served amazing food but also stood for something much deeper. Newt and Kraus ended up landing on a mission to reward the public service sector

---

101. http://www.hardrockhotels.com/thesoundofyourstay.htm

for their protection and aptly named the restaurant, Mission BBQ. Mission defines their purpose as:

To support our local police, fire departments, and armed services, Mission collects donations and constantly holds special events. This has allowed Mission to raise tens of thousands of dollars for numerous noteworthy causes and organizations, including the Wounded Warrior Project, the USO, and Toys for Tots.

Bill Krause elaborated on the mission by saying, "Our mission at Mission BBQ is to serve. The world didn't need another restaurant, but maybe it needed a place that stands for what's right and that makes you feel good if you have served or are serving."

7. **Follow-up (maintenance)** - Doing the little extra to follow-up with your franchisees or customers.

Example: Mitchell's

When was the last time you personally thanked a customer? Sent a hand-written note? Each year Jack Mitchell writes over 1,700 personal notes to customers of his retail stores[102]. That's about five notes a day, every day. Mitchell is CEO of The Mitchells Family of Stores, which owns several high-end retail stores, including Marsh, Mitchells, and Richards and is author of *Hug Your Customers.*

8. **Added Service (maintenance)** - The little extra that's an added unexpected service.

Example: Safelite

Safelite does a little extra, and it doesn't cost them a single penny to do it. After replacing your damaged window, Safelite Auto Glass simply cleans your windows, vacuums up any glass fragments, and

---

102. http://www.1to1media.com/customer-engagement/customer-experience-balancing-high-touch-and-high-tech

sends you on your way with one less thing to worry about. Getting auto glass replaced doesn't have to be a big headache—and Safelite proves that with their outstanding customer service. By taking care of all the worries that surround a window replacement on a vehicle, Safelite is one giant leap ahead of their competition.

9. Convenience (maintenance) - The little extras you add to make things easier for your customers.

Example: TD Bank

A lot of companies like to lay the claim of being customer-centric, though not many live up to the hype. Little actions speak far louder than words ever could. TD Bank not only has longer hours than other banks but they're also open seven days a week. In addition, they've pulled together a number of ways to communicate that they care about their customers including automated thanking machines and throwback Thursdays.

10. Waiting (maintenance) - All customers hate to wait. If it's inevitable, how can you do a little extra to make it more bearable?

Example: Lexus

Lexus makes waiting enjoyable. In the words of Carolyn Ray, "At Lexus of North Miami, people who come in for service are entitled to a complimentary spa service at their in-house spa. Services include manicures, pedicures, haircuts, waxing, or chair massage. There is a full-service cafe, kids playroom, and fitness center for waiting customers. Makes coming in for service a total pleasure!"

11. Special Needs (maintenance) - Acknowledging that some customers have needs that require special attention.

Example: Rainforest Cafe

Rainforest Cafe goes above and beyond for customers with food allergies. Servers are proactive by asking, "Does anybody have any food allergies we should know about?" The restaurant has a separate menu that covers many of the allergy concerns guests have.

12. Handling Mistakes (maintenance) - Admitting that you're wrong and doing the little extra above and beyond to make it "more than right."

Example: Nurse Next Door

This home healthcare provider has an interesting way of handling mistakes with customers. And let's face it, we all make mistakes. It's how you handle them that makes all the difference. In addition to sending a handwritten note, Nurse Next Door sends a freshly baked apple pie to apologize. Literally, a humble pie.

When a franchise applies the SYSTEM and utilizes some of the 12 Types of Purple Goldfish to establish points of difference to their competitors and to create compelling paths for the franchisee to demonstrate their emotional passion, then we have a win-win-win! A trifecta win creates a win for the customer, the franchisee, and the franchisor!

ADDITIONAL INSPIRATION AND RECOMMENDED READING

Other books that we highly recommend:

- *Delivering Happiness* by Tony Hsieh
- *Hug Your Customers* by Jack Mitchell
- *The Next Evolution of Marketing* by Bob Gilbreath
- *Jab, Jab, Jab, Right Hook* by Gary Vaynerchuk
- *The Experience Effect* by Jim Joseph
- *Purple Cow* by Seth Godin
- *It's My Pleasure* by Dee Ann Turner
- *Domino* by Linda Ireland
- *My Story* by Stew Leonard
- *FREE* by Chris Anderson
- *Winning the Customer* by Lou Imbriano
- *99.3 Random Acts of Marketing* by Drew McLellan
- *Five Star Customer Service* by Ted Coiné
- *The End of Business as Usual* by Brian Solis
- *BAM* by Barry Moltz

- *Killing Giants* by Stephen Denny
- *Tipping Point* by Malcolm Gladwell
- *The New Rules of Marketing & PR* by David Meerman Scott
- *The Customer Rules: The 39 Essential Rules for Delivering Essential Service* by Lee Cockerell
- *Be Our Guest: Perfecting the Art of Customer Service* by The Disney Institute Theodore Kinni
- *Uplifting Service: The Proven Path to Delighting Your Customers* by Ron Kaufman
- *Return on Relationship* by Kathryn Rose and Ted Rubin
- *Freak Factor* by David Rendall
- *Uncommon Service* by Frances Frei and Anne Morriss
- *Be Your Customers Hero* by Adam Toporek
- *The Power of Moments* by Chip and Dan Heath

ABOUT THE AUTHORS

STAN PHELPS

Stan Phelps is a best-selling author, keynote speaker, and workshop facilitator. He believes that today's organizations must focus on meaningful differentiation to win the hearts of both employees and customers.

He is the founder of PurpleGoldfish.com. Purple Goldfish is a think tank of customer experience and employee engagement experts that offers keynotes and workshops that drive loyalty and sales. The group helps organizations connect with the hearts and minds of customers and employees.

Prior to PurpleGoldfish.com, Stan had a 20-year career in marketing that included leadership positions at IMG, adidas, PGA Exhibitions, and Synergy. At Synergy, he worked on award-winning experiential programs for top brands such as KFC, Wachovia, NASCAR, Starbucks, and M&M's.

Stan is a TEDx speaker, a Forbes contributor, and IBM Futurist. His writing is syndicated on top sites such as Customer Think and Business2Community. He has spoken at over 300 events across locations that include Australia, Bahrain, Canada, Ecuador, France, Germany, Holland, Israel, Japan, Malaysia, Peru, Sweden, Russia, Spain, UK, and the U.S.

He is the author of eight other books:

- *Purple Goldfish - 12 Ways to Win Customers and Influence Word of Mouth*

- *Green Goldfish - 15 Ways to Drive Employee Engagement and Reinforce Culture*
- *Golden Goldfish - The Vital Few*
- *Blue Goldfish - Using Technology, Data, and Analytics to Drive Both Profits & Prophets*
- *Purple Goldfish Service Edition - 12 Ways Hotels, Restaurants & Airlines Win the Right Customers*
- *Red Goldfish - Motivating Sales and Loyalty Through Shared Passion and Purpose*
- *Bar Tricks, Bad Jokes, and Even Worse Stories*
- *Pink Goldfish - Defy Normal, Exploit Imperfection and Captivate Your Customers*

Stan received a BS in Marketing and Human Resources from Marist College, a JD/MBA from Villanova University, and a certificate for Achieving Breakthrough Service from Harvard Business School. He is a Certified Net Promoter Associate and has taught as an adjunct professor at NYU, Rutgers University, and Manhattanville College. Stan lives in Cary, North Carolina, with his wife, Jennifer and two boys, Thomas & James.

Stan is also a fellow at Maddock Douglas, an innovation consulting firm in Chicago.

To book Stan for an upcoming keynote, webinar, or workshop, go stanphelpsspeaks.com. You can reach Stan at stan@purplegoldfish.com or call +1.919.360.4702.

TIFFANY W. DODSON

Tiffany bought her first franchise 14 years ago. She was working 80-hour weeks as a senior brand manager on one of the world's largest brands when her two toddlers delivered a "wake-up call." Exploring her options, Tiffany decided that entrepreneurship with the financial rewards and lifestyle flexibility best suited her career and life goals.

Tiffany has deep roots in the franchise industry. She has held senior marketing roles at well-known international franchises, including an international food franchisor. Furthermore, she is recognized not only as a top performing franchisee, but also as a top master franchisee and was voted by her peers to be the Master Developer, not once but twice in an international franchise. In the span of eight years, Tiffany grew her master franchise areas from four locations to 90.

With a passion for franchises and small businesses, Tiffany uses her business knowledge and experience to coach other business owners so that they too achieve their dream.

Tiffany moved back to her hometown of Winston-Salem, North Carolina, over ten years ago with her husband Ryan and two daughters, Willard and Ritter. The family spends a lot of time at horse barns, music concerts, and traveling both in the U.S. and abroad. Five times a week Tiffany spends quality time with a personal trainer, "training for life."

To book Tiffany for an upcoming keynote, webinar, or workshop, go to purplegoldfish.com. You can reach her at tiffany@tiffanywdodson.com or call +1.336.306.3578.

OTHER COLORS IN THE GOLDFISH SERIES

PURPLE GOLDFISH
12 WAYS TO WIN CUSTOMERS AND INFLUENCE WORD OF MOUTH

This book is based on the Purple Goldfish Project, a crowdsourcing effort that collected more than 1,001 examples of signature-added value. The book draws inspiration from the concept of lagniappe, providing 12 practical strategies for winning the hearts of customers and influencing positive word of mouth.

GREEN GOLDFISH
BEYOND DOLLARS: 15 WAYS TO DRIVE EMPLOYEE ENGAGEMENT AND REINFORCE CULTURE

Green Goldfish examines the importance of employee engagement in today's workplace. The book showcases 15 signature ways to increase employee engagement beyond compensation to reinforce the culture of an organization.

GOLDEN GOLDFISH
THE VITAL FEW: ALL CUSTOMERS AND EMPLOYEES ARE NOT CREATED EQUAL

Golden Goldfish examines the importance of your top 20 percent of customers and employees. The book showcases nine ways to drive loyalty and retention with these two critical groups.

BLUE GOLDFISH

USING TECHNOLOGY, DATA, AND ANALYTICS TO DRIVE BOTH PROFITS AND PROPHETS

Blue Goldfish examines how to leverage technology, data, and analytics to do a "little something extra" to improve the experience for the customer. The book is based on a collection of over 300 case studies. It examines the three R's: Relationship, Responsiveness, and Readiness. Blue Goldfish also uncovers eight different ways to turn insights into action.

RED GOLDFISH

MOTIVATING SALES AND LOYALTY THROUGH SHARED PASSION AND PURPOSE

Purpose is changing the way we work and how customers choose business partners. It is driving loyalty, and it's on its way to becoming the ultimate differentiator in business. Red Goldfish shares cutting edge examples and reveals the eight ways businesses can embrace purpose that drives employee engagement, fuels the bottom line, and makes an impact on the lives of those it serves.

PURPLE GOLDFISH SERVICE EDITION

12 WAYS HOTELS, RESTAURANTS, AND AIRLINES WIN THE RIGHT CUSTOMERS

Purple Goldfish Service Edition is about differentiation via added value. Marketing to your existing customers via G.L.U.E. (giving little unexpected extras). Packed with over 100 examples, the book focuses on the 12 ways to do the "little extras" to improve the customer experience for restaurants, hotels, and airlines. The end result is increased sales, happier customers, and positive word of mouth.

PINK GOLDFISH

DEFY ORDINARY, EXPLOIT IMPERFECTION, AND CAPTIVATE YOUR CUSTOMERS

Companies need to stand out in a crowded marketplace, but true differentiation is increasingly rare. Based on over 200 case studies, Pink Goldfish provides an unconventional seven-part framework for achieving competitive separation by embracing flaws, instead of fixing them.

YELLOW GOLDFISH

NINE WAYS TO INCREASE HAPPINESS IN BUSINESS TO DRIVE GROWTH, PRODUCTIVITY, AND PROSPERITY

There should be only one metric for success in business and that's providing/creating happiness. A yellow goldfish is anytime a business does a little extra to contribute to the happiness of its customers, employees, or society. Based on over 250 case studies, Yellow Goldfish provides a nine-part framework for happiness driven growth, productivity, and prosperity in business.

27119803R00109

Made in the USA
Columbia, SC
20 September 2018